TABLE OF CONTENTS

TABLE OF CONTENTS, CONTINUED

The American Vision

Graphic Organizer Transparencies, Strategies, and Activities

Glencoe

New York, New York   Columbus, Ohio   Chicago, Illinois   Peoria, Illinois   Woodland Hills, California

The McGraw·Hill Companies

Send all inquiries to:
Glencoe/McGraw-Hill
8787 Orion Place
Columbus, Ohio 43240

ISBN 0-07-868080-8

Printed in the United States of America

2 3 4 5 6 7 8 9 10 081 10 09 08 07 06 05

TABLE OF CONTENTS, CONTINUED

Transparencies

Graphic Organizer 1   Main Idea Chart
Graphic Organizer 2   K-W-L-H Chart
Graphic Organizer 3   Web Diagram
Graphic Organizer 4   Tree Diagram
Graphic Organizer 5   Venn Diagram
Graphic Organizer 6   Table or Matrix
Graphic Organizer 7   Table
Graphic Organizer 8   Table: Pyramid
Graphic Organizer 9   Fishbone Diagram
Graphic Organizer 10   Horizontal Time Line
Graphic Organizer 11   Vertical Time Line
Graphic Organizer 12   Problem-Solution Chart
Graphic Organizer 13   Cause-Effect Chart
Graphic Organizer 14   Cause-Effect Chart
Graphic Organizer 15   Chain-of-Events or Flowchart

TO THE TEACHER

Graphic organizers are visual representations of written material. Charts, graphs, diagrams, and maps are all examples of graphic organizers. The use of graphic organizers promotes reading and thinking. In addition, writing information in a visual or an illustrated way helps students to clarify and categorize it for easier recall. It also helps students see connections among parallel or related facts. Finally, many teachers believe that having students list information in a graphic organizer makes learning more fun than just taking notes in the traditional way.

This booklet provides you with more than 125 Graphic Organizer Teaching Strategies—at least one for every section of *The American Vision*. In addition, a reproducible Student Activity—utilizing a graphic organizer—is provided for each chapter. The activities are designed to help students efficiently organize their study of each chapter in particular, and to organize and improve their note-taking skills and study habits in general.

About the Teaching Strategies

Each Graphic Organizer Teaching Strategy follows the same basic format:
- A listed objective explains what the student is expected to do.
- The number of the Graphic Organizer Transparency or reproducible graphic organizer (from the Graphic Organizer Library) that corresponds to the Teaching Strategy is given. You are to project or photocopy that particular graphic organizer and distribute copies of it to students before they begin the activity.
- A list of steps is then provided, as well as page numbers from *The American Vision* from which students will gather information to complete the steps.
- A summary statement or discussion idea may be used as a review for students.

Presenting the Student Activity

One of the Graphic Organizer Teaching Strategies for each chapter is tied to the Student Activity that directly follows the Teaching Strategy page. Answers to the Student Activity are provided.

Before requiring students to complete a Student Activity, describe the purpose of the particular graphic organizer. Demonstrate how to use the textbook and prior knowledge to fill in information in the various parts of the graphic organizer. Provide opportunities for students to work in groups as well as individually when completing the graphic organizers, which will teach students to analyze the graphic more closely. Finally, after students have completed the Student Activity, discuss the responses as a class. This will help students learn to revise their thought processes and better clarify the organization of their graphic organizers.

Graphic Organizer Library

In addition to Teaching Strategies, Student Activities, and the Graphic Organizer Transparencies, this booklet contains 15 reproducible graphic organizers on pages 1–15. They correspond directly to the Graphic Organizer Transparencies and are utilized throughout the Graphic Organizer Teaching Strategies.

Each type of graphic organizer is best suited for a specific kind or purpose of visual presentation. For example, one type of graphic organizer may be better suited to categorize information sequentially; another to compare and/or contrast; a third to describe, support, or exemplify a main idea; and so on. The following information will explain for what purpose each of the graphic organizers in the Graphic Organizer Library is best suited.

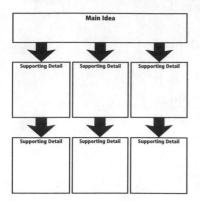

Graphic Organizer 1:
Main Idea Chart
This type of graphic organizer is helpful when you want students to find the main idea of a paragraph or section, and then to analyze the reading further for more information that exemplifies and/or supports that main idea.

Graphic Organizer 2:
K-W-L-H Chart
The K-W-L-H chart is used to activate students' prior knowledge and interest before they read as well as to set a purpose for reading. This chart asks for student feedback on what they *Know* already, what they *Want* to find out, what they *Learned,* and *How* they can learn more.

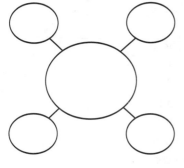

Graphic Organizer 3:
Web Diagram
Web diagrams are often used to help students identify one central idea and organize related information around it. Students must determine the broad categories that should be listed in the outer parts of the web. Then students must determine what is relevant factual material and group this data into the appropriate related categories.

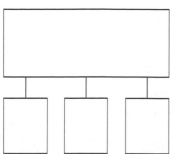

Graphic Organizer 4:
Tree Diagram
A tree diagram is based upon the traditional "family tree" organizational graphic. Students are required to record how subordinate facts or statements are related to one another and to a larger, unifying statement. Tree diagrams may also be utilized as a main idea/supporting details type of graphic organizer.

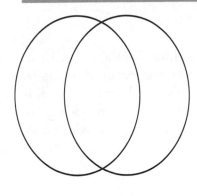

Graphic Organizer 5:
Venn Diagram
Venn diagrams are used to compare and contrast information or to show similarities and differences among various objects or subjects. The Venn diagram consists of two or more overlapping circles. Differences are listed in the outer parts of the circles. Similarities are described where the circles overlap. Venn diagrams are especially helpful in displaying similarities and differences at a glance.

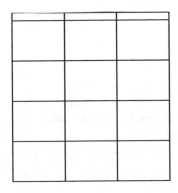

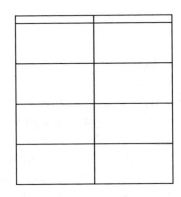

Graphic Organizers 6 and 7:
Table or Matrix
Tables and matrices are used to organize or categorize information or make comparisons among categories. The items to be compared are listed along the left side of the table's rows, and the general features are listed across the top of the table before filling in the cells with facts or supporting information. Graphic Organizer 7 may also be used as a storyboard.

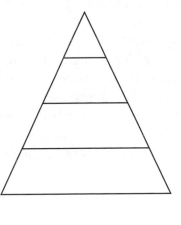

Graphic Organizer 8:
Table: Pyramid
A pyramid table is very effective for organizing information in a majority/minority or general-to-specific manner. A pyramid table can also be used to list details or facts leading up to a climax or culminating event.

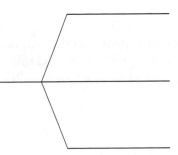

Graphic Organizer 9:
Fishbone Diagram
The purpose of a fishbone diagram is very similar to that of a main idea/supporting details chart. A main idea statement or category is written on the single line to the left. Supporting facts, examples, or subcategories are written on the lines to the right. In many cases, a third set of lines can be generated and attached to the subcategories with additional information or facts.

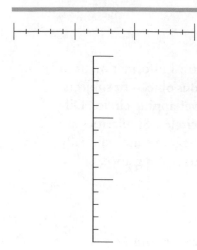

Graphic Organizers 10 and 11:
Horizontal and Vertical Time Lines

Time lines are used to list important dates in chronological order. Horizontal and vertical time lines require students to analyze information by sequencing events. Time lines also require students to determine baseline dates and to be cognizant of the "backward" nature of B.C. chronology. In addition, the horizontal time line may be used as a rating scale continuum on which students may rate low and high points.

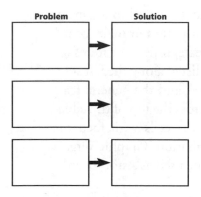

Graphic Organizer 12:
Problem-Solution Chart

The purpose of this type of graphic organizer is to help students streamline the steps involved in recognizing a problem and utilizing problem-solving skills. The problem-solution chart may be best suited for group discussion after the teacher has explained an event or action. Students may then describe or predict the problem, after which they may brainstorm multiple solutions and possible results of those solutions.

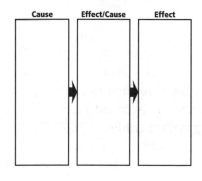

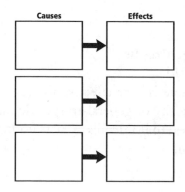

Graphic Organizers 13 and 14:
Cause–Effect Charts

This type of organizer helps students analyze information by identifying cause-and-effect relationships. In some cases, students will identify separate causes and their effects. In other instances, students may be required to identify a sequence of a cause and its effect, which becomes the cause of yet another effect.

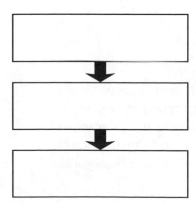

Graphic Organizer 15:
Chain-of-Events or Flowchart

A chain-of-events or flowchart asks students to organize and interpret information by sequencing the stages of an event. This type of graphic organizer is also used to describe the actions of a character or group, or the steps to be followed in a procedure.

Graphic Organizer 1: Main Idea Chart

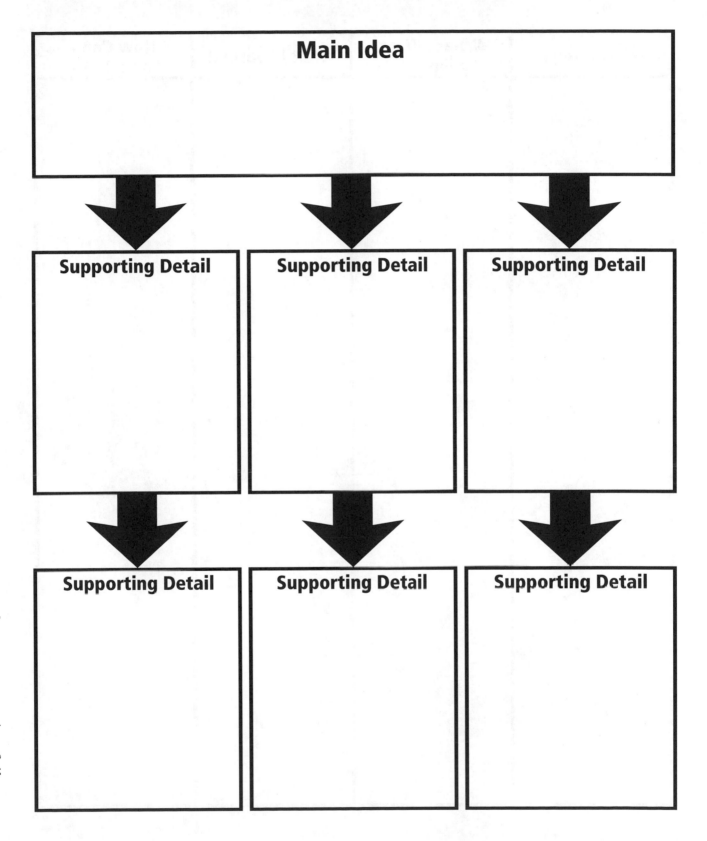

Graphic Organizer 2: K-W-L-H Chart

What I Know	What I Want to Find Out	What I Learned	How Can I Learn More

Graphic Organizer 3: Web Diagram

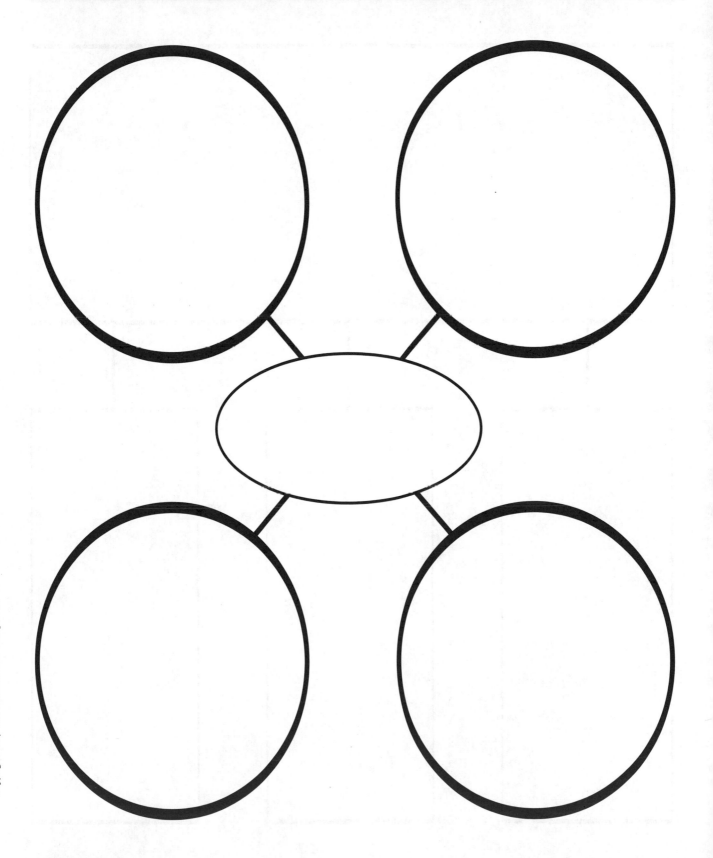

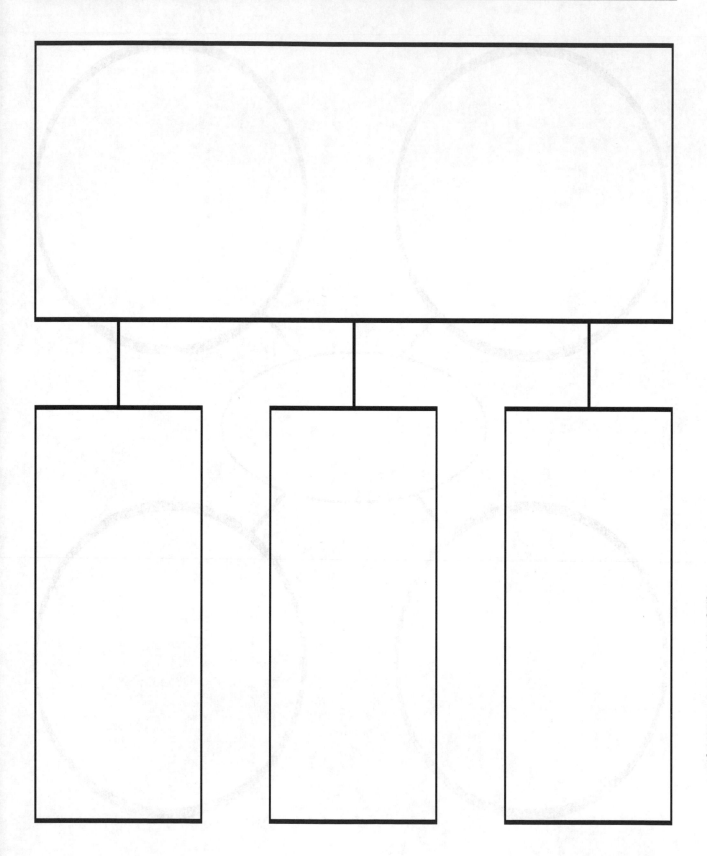

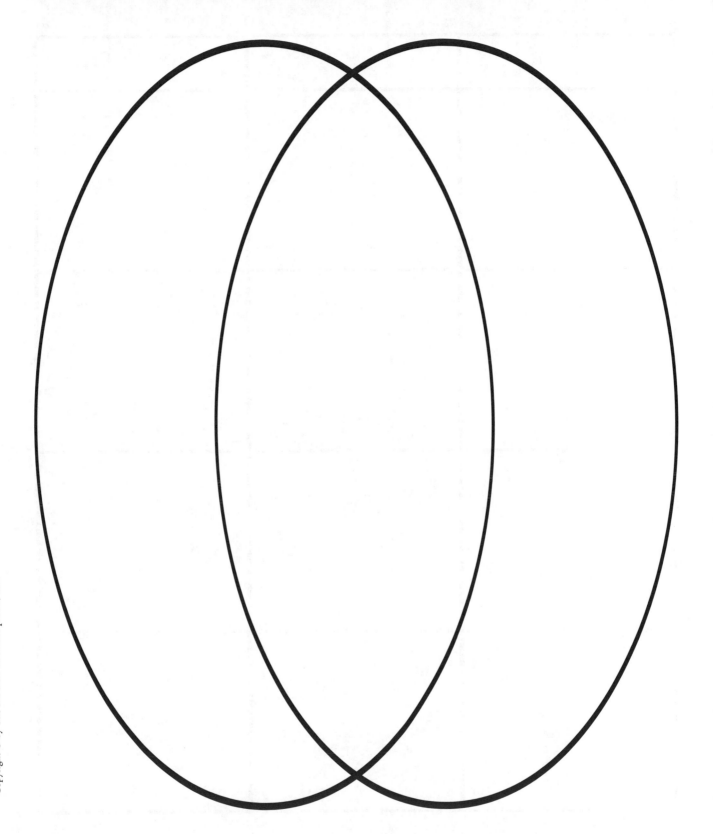

Graphic Organizer 6: Table or Matrix

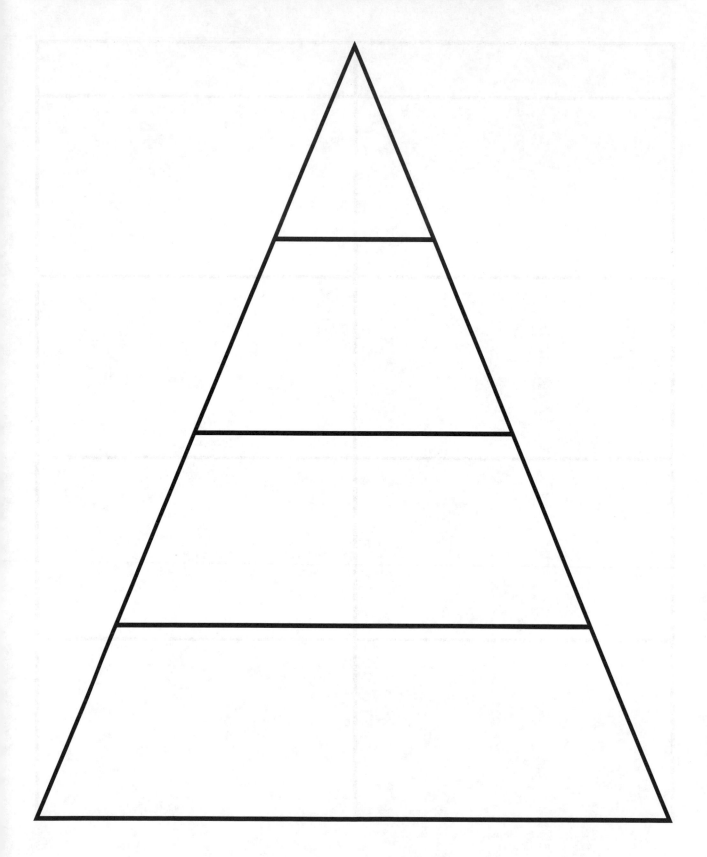

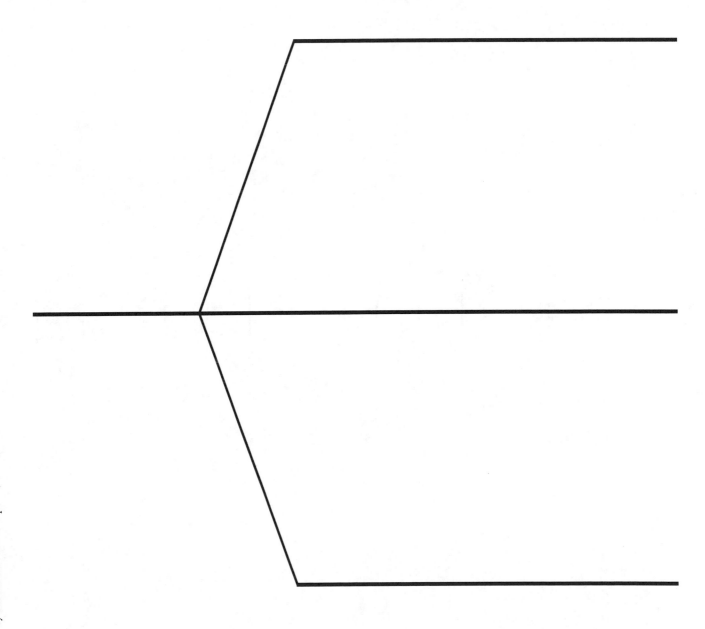

Graphic Organizer 10: Horizontal Time Line

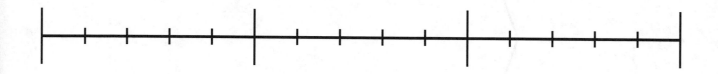

Graphic Organizer 11: Vertical Time Line

Graphic Organizer 12: Problem-Solution Chart

Problem

Solution

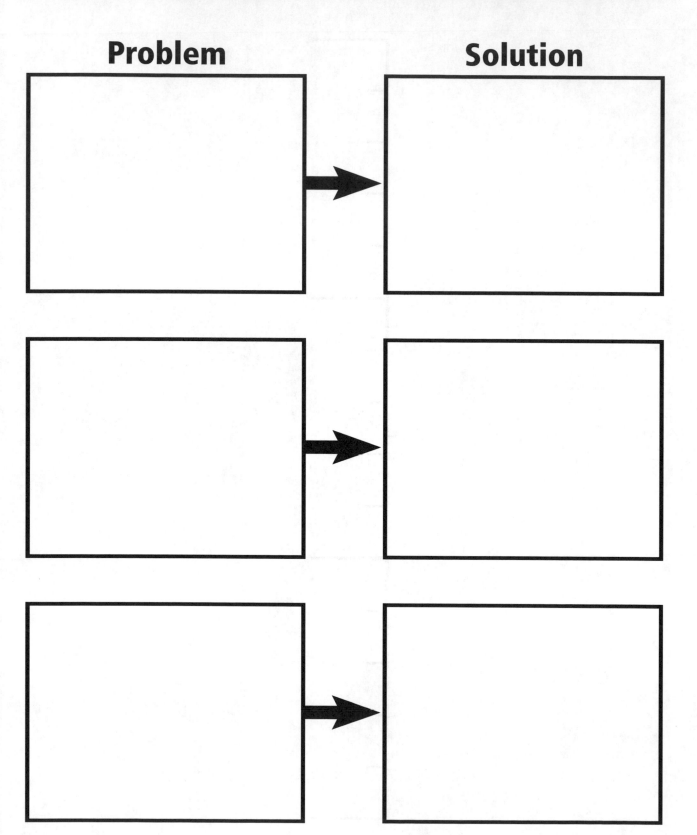

Graphic Organizer 13: Cause–Effect Chart

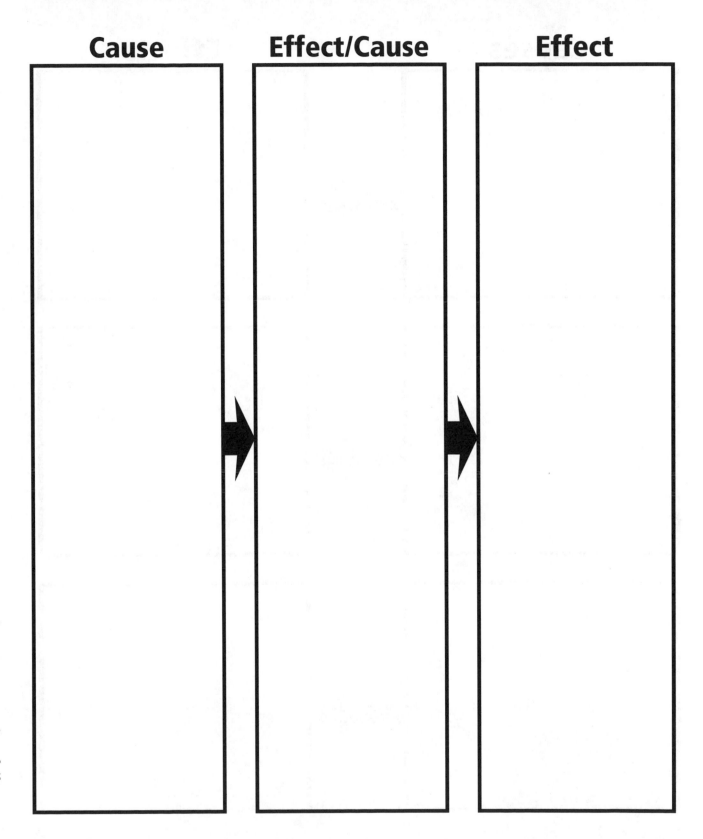

Cause

Effect/Cause

Effect

Graphic Organizer 14: Cause–Effect Chart

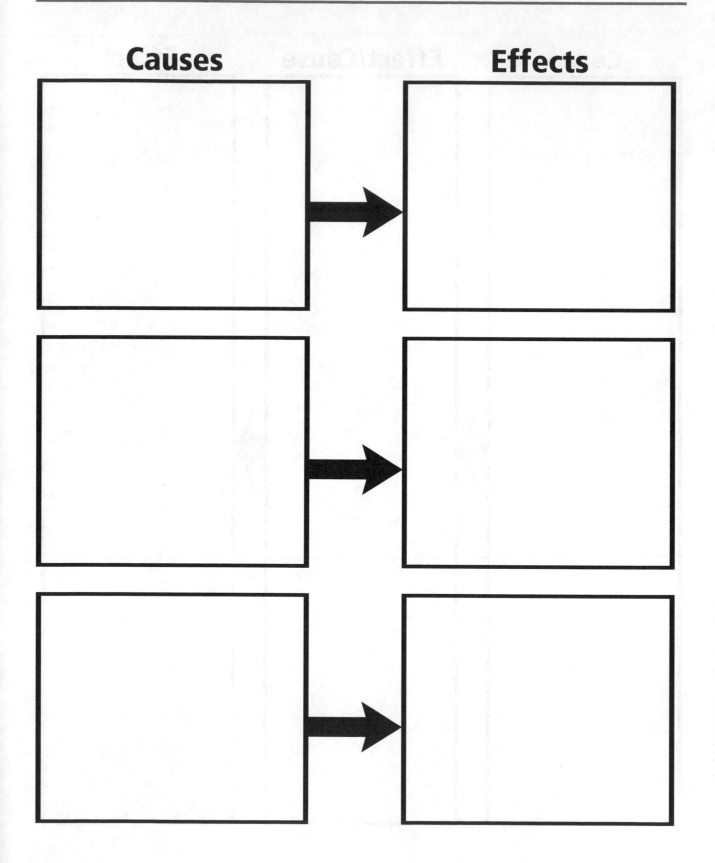

Causes

Effects

Graphic Organizer 15: Chain-of-Events or Flowchart

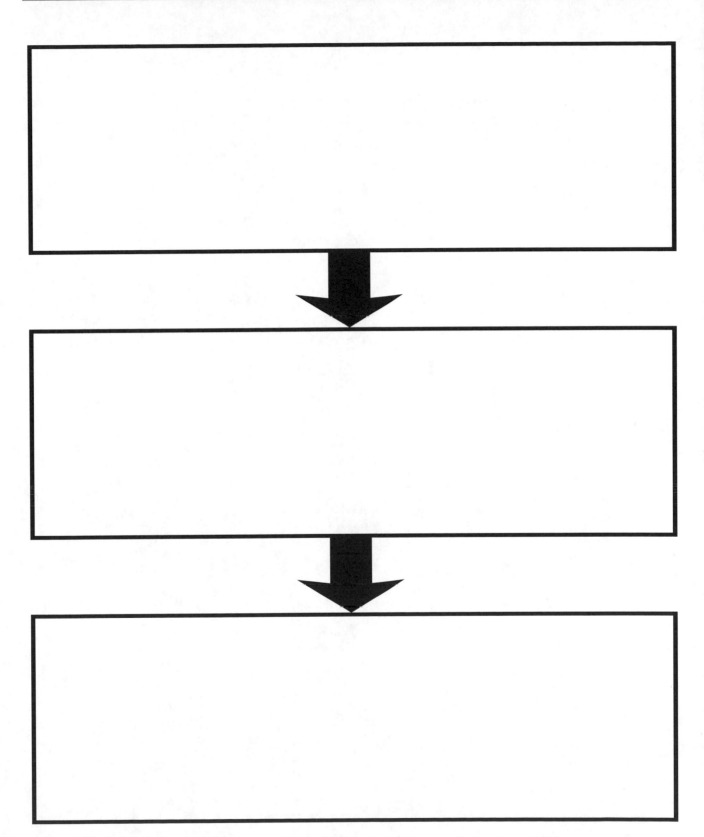

Graphic Organizer Strategies

Use with Chapter 1

Web Diagram
Teaching Strategy *(Use with Section 1)*

OBJECTIVE: The student will identify a central idea and organize related information around it.

➯ Use with Graphic Organizer 3—Web Diagram.

- Present Graphic Organizer Transparency 3 or reproduce Graphic Organizer 3. Explain the objective above.
- Have students write the main idea, **North American Cultures,** in the center circle of the diagram. Tell students to read "North American Cultures" in Section 1, pages 15–17. As students read, ask them to list and describe four North American cultures in the four outer circles.
- Discuss the web diagrams with the students.

PRESENTING STUDENT ACTIVITY 1

Main Idea Chart Teaching Strategy and Student Activity *(Use with Section 2)*

➯ Please note: The Main Idea Teaching Strategy corresponds with Graphic Organizer 1.

OBJECTIVE: The student will find information that supports the main idea.

Reproduce and distribute Student Activity 1. Tell students to analyze the reading for information that supports the main idea: **The Native Americans of what is today the United States had diverse ways of life.** Have students list six supporting facts in the six boxes.

Answers to Student Activity 1

Answers may include the following: **Southwest**—when a man married, he joined the household of his wife; men's and women's work was separate; boys joined kachina cult; **Pacific Coast**—some lived in permanent settlements; others were nomadic; **Great Plains**—until 1500 were farmers, after 1500 became nomads who lived in teepees; **Far North**—hunted seals and walruses; invented devices to cope with harsh environment; lived in groups; **Eastern Woodlands**—hunted, fished, farmed; used several types of houses; made wampum.

Fishbone Diagram
Teaching Strategy *(Use with Section 3)*

OBJECTIVE: The student will organize a main idea and supporting facts.

➯ Use with Graphic Organizer 9—Fishbone Diagram.

- Present Graphic Organizer Transparency 9 or reproduce Graphic Organizer 9. Explain the objective above.
- Tell students to write the main idea, **Three Great Empires rose and fell in West Africa between the 400s and 1500s,** on the single line on the left of the diagram. Have students read "The Empires of West Africa" from Section 3, pages 27–29.
- As students read, tell them to list and describe the three empires of West Africa on the three lines on the right.

Chain-of-Events or Flowchart
Teaching Strategy *(Use with Section 4)*

OBJECTIVE: The student will identify events or steps leading up to a final outcome.

➯ Use with Graphic Organizer 15—Chain-of-Events or Flowchart.

- Present Graphic Organizer Transparency 15 or reproduce Graphic Organizer 15. Tell students that they will use this chain-of-events chart to show the events that occurred as a result of the Crusades.
- Tell students to read Section 4, pages 32–37, and list events that happened as a result of the Crusades.
- Discuss students' chain-of-events charts.

Tree Diagram
Teaching Strategy *(Use with Section 5)*

OBJECTIVE: The student will analyze information by identifying the main idea and supporting details.

➯ Use with Graphic Organizer 4—Tree Diagram.

- Present Graphic Organizer Transparency 4 or reproduce Graphic Organizer 4. Tell students that tree diagrams are used to record how facts are related to one another.
- Tell students to read "Spain Sends Columbus West" in Section 5, pages 39–41. Have students list three outcomes of Columbus's journeys to the Americas in the three lower boxes on the tree. Then ask students to write a title for the tree diagram in the large box at the top.
- Have students explain their diagrams to the class.

Converging Cultures, Prehistory to 1520 | **GRAPHIC ORGANIZER ACTIVITY 1**

Diverse Native Americans

Directions: Find information in your reading that supports the main idea listed in the top box, "The Native Americans of what is today the United States had diverse ways of life." List six supporting facts in the six boxes below.

Main Idea

The Native Americans of what is today the United States had diverse ways of life.

| **Supporting Detail** | **Supporting Detail** | **Supporting Detail** |

| **Supporting Detail** | **Supporting Detail** | **Supporting Detail** |

Graphic Organizer Strategies

Use with Chapter 2

PRESENTING STUDENT ACTIVITY 2
K-W-L-H Chart Teaching Strategy and Student Activity *(Use with Section 1)*

▮▮▶ Please note: The K-W-L-H Chart Teaching Strategy corresponds with Graphic Organizer 2, found in the Graphic Organizer Library.

OBJECTIVE: Students will list what they know about the Spanish and French colonies in America, discover what information they do not know, and then learn that new information.

Reproduce and distribute Student Activity 2. Tell students that they are to list what they already know about the Spanish and French colonies in the first column. Suggest to students that they think about the values of European society and the geography of the regions in which Europeans settled, and any additional facts that they may know about Spanish and French colonies. In the next column, they are to list what they want to find out about the Spanish and French colonies in America. Students are to complete the chart after reading Section 1, pages 50–57, to see what they have learned about the Spanish and French colonies in America and how they can learn more. Discuss completed charts with students.

Answers to Student Activity 2
Student answers will vary. Check facts for accuracy.

Fishbone Diagram Teaching Strategy *(Use with Section 2)*

OBJECTIVE: The student will organize a main idea and supporting facts.

▮▮▶ Use with Graphic Organizer 9—Fishbone Diagram—from the Graphic Organizer Library.

• Present Graphic Organizer Transparency 9 or reproduce Graphic Organizer 9. Tell students that tree diagrams are used to record how facts are related to one another.
• Tell students to write the main idea, **Religious, economic, and political changes in England led to the founding of the first English colonies in America,** on the single line on the left of the diagram. Have students read "England Takes Interest in America" in Section 2, pages 58–61. Ask them to list three causes of the founding of English colonies in America on the three lines on the right.
• Discuss completed diagrams with the students.

Table or Matrix Teaching Strategy *(Use with Section 3)*

OBJECTIVE: The student will categorize information in a table.

▮▮▶ Use with Graphic Organizer 6—Table or Matrix—from the Graphic Organizer Library.

• Present Graphic Organizer Transparency 6 or reproduce Graphic Organizer 6. Tell students that they will use this table to describe the New England colonies of **Massachusetts, Rhode Island, Connecticut, New Hampshire,** and **Maine.**
• Students are to list these colonies on the left side of their table, outside of the table. Under each column heading on their table, they are to label **Date Founded, Who Founded, Reasons Founded.**
• Ask students to read Section 3, pages 66–71. They are to locate the corresponding information about each colony and list that information under the proper heading.

Table Teaching Strategy *(Use with Section 4)*

OBJECTIVE: The student will compile and organize information on a table.

▮▮▶ Use with Graphic Organizer 7—Table—from the Graphic Organizer Library.

• Present Graphic Organizer Transparency 7 or reproduce Graphic Organizer 7. Tell students that they will use this table to show information about the Middle and Southern Colonies.
• Instruct students to label the columns with the two headings: **Middle Colonies** and **Southern Colonies.**
• As students read Section 4, pages 72–77, they are to list details under the proper headings describing the colonies.
• Discuss with students the similarities and differences between the two groups of colonies.

GRAPHIC ORGANIZER ACTIVITY 2

Spanish and French Colonies in America

Directions: List what you already know about the Spanish and French colonies in America under the "What I Know" column on the chart below. Think about the values of European society and the geography of the regions in which the Spanish and French settled, and any additional facts that you may know. In the next column, list questions that you may want to find out as you read Section 1, on pages 50–57 of your textbook. Complete the chart after reading Section 1 to see what you have learned about the Spanish and French colonies and how you can learn more.

What I Know	What I Want to Find Out	What I Learned	How Can I Learn More

Use with Chapter 3

PRESENTING STUDENT ACTIVITY 3
Web Diagram Teaching Strategy and Student Activity *(Use with Section 1)*

▥▶ Please note: The Web Diagram Teaching Strategy corresponds with Graphic Organizer 3, found in the Graphic Organizer Library.

OBJECTIVE: The student will identify one central idea and organize related information around it.

Reproduce and distribute Student Activity 3. Tell students that they will use this web diagram to describe the society that emerged in the Southern Colonies. As students read "Southern Society" in Section 1, pages 86–87 of their textbooks, they are to list four social classes that emerged in the Southern Colonies.

Discuss with students the way of life of the people in each social class.

Answers to Student Activity 3
planter elite; backcountry farmers or yeomen; landless tenant farmers; servants, enslaved African Americans; Descriptions will vary.

Venn Diagram
Teaching Strategy *(Use with Section 2)*

OBJECTIVE: The student will analyze information by comparing and contrasting.

▥▶ Use with Graphic Organizer 5—Venn Diagram—from the Graphic Organizer Library.

- Present Graphic Organizer Transparency 5 or reproduce Graphic Organizer 5. Tell students that Venn diagrams are used to compare and contrast two items. In this activity, students will use the diagram to show differences and similarities between the New England and Middle Colonies.
- Tell students to label the outer circles **Middle Colonies** and **New England Colonies,** and label the overlapping part **Both.**
- Have students read Section 2 on pages 91–97. They are to list facts unique to each colony in the outer circles. Then

students should list any similarities between the two colonies in the overlapping part.
- Discuss the completed diagrams with the students.

Chain-of-Events or Flowchart
Teaching Strategy *(Use with Section 3)*

OBJECTIVE: The student will identify events or steps leading up to a final outcome.

▥▶ Use with Graphic Organizer 15—Chain-of-Events or Flowchart—from the Graphic Organizer Library.

- Present Graphic Organizer Transparency 15 or reproduce Graphic Organizer 15. Tell students that they will use this chain-of-events chart to show the events that led up to the Glorious Revolution in America.
- After student have read "The Glorious Revolution of 1688" in Section 3, pages 100–102, tell them to list events that led up to the Glorious Revolution in America.

Fishbone Diagram
Teaching Strategy *(Use with Section 4)*

OBJECTIVE: The student will organize a main idea and supporting facts.

▥▶ Use with Graphic Organizer 9—Fishbone Diagram—from the Graphic Organizer Library.

- Present Graphic Organizer Transparency 9 or reproduce Graphic Organizer 9. Tell students that fishbone diagrams are used to organize main ideas and supporting facts.
- Tell students to write the main idea, **Enslaved African Americans' Forms of Resistance,** on the single line on the left of the diagram. Have students read "Africans in Colonial America" in Section 4, pages 106–107.
- As students read, tell them to list three forms of resistance by enslaved African Americans on the three lines on the right of the diagram.
- Discuss with students the plight of enslaved African Americans and their methods of resistance.

Colonial Ways of Life, 1607–1763   **GRAPHIC ORGANIZER ACTIVITY 3**

Ways of Life in Southern Colonies

Directions: Read "Southern Society" in Section 3 on pages 86–87 of your textbook. As you read, list and describe four social classes that emerged in the Southern Colonies.

Southern Society

The American Vision

Use with Chapter 4

Main Idea Chart
Teaching Strategy *(Use with Section 1)*

OBJECTIVE: The student will interpret information from the text by identifying the main idea and supporting details.

⟩ Use with Graphic Organizer 1—Main Idea Chart—from the Graphic Organizer Library.

• Present Graphic Organizer Transparency 1 or reproduce Graphic Organizer 1. Tell students that on this chart, they will list significant details that support the following main idea: **The policies Britain adopted to gain greater control over its North American empire caused increased tension between the British and the colonists.**

• Have students read "The Colonies Grow Discontented" in Section 1 on pages 119–123. As they read, students are to list significant details from the text that support the main idea.

• Discuss students' main idea charts after they have completed the activity.

Cause-Effect Chart
Teaching Strategy *(Use with Section 2)*

OBJECTIVE: The student will analyze information by identifying cause-and-effect relationships.

⟩ Use with Graphic Organizer 2—Cause-Effect Chart—from the Graphic Organizer Library.

• Present Graphic Organizer Transparency 2 or reproduce Graphic Organizer 2. Tell students that they will use this chart to show three causes and their effects.

• Have students write the following statements inside the Cause boxes: **Parliament passed the Tea Act of 1773; Parliament passed the Intolerable Acts; Thomas Paine published *Common Sense.***

• Tell students to read Section 2 on pages 126–133. As they read, they are to complete the Effects boxes on their charts.

• Discuss the cause-and-effect relationships with students.

Chain-of-Events or Flowchart
Teaching Strategy *(Use with Section 3)*

OBJECTIVE: The student will identify events or steps leading up to a final outcome.

⟩ Use with Graphic Organizer 15—Chain-of-Events or Flowchart—from the Graphic Organizer Library.

• Present Graphic Organizer Transparency 15 or reproduce Graphic Organizer 15. Tell students that they will use this chain-of-events chart to show the events that led up to the Treaty of Paris.

• After students have read Section 3 on pages 138–145, tell them to list major events in the War for Independence that finally led to the Treaty of Paris.

PRESENTING STUDENT ACTIVITY 4
Tree Diagram Teaching Strategy and Student Activity *(Use with Section 4)*

⟩ Please note: The Tree Diagram Teaching Strategy corresponds with Graphic Organizer 4, found in the Graphic Organizer Library.

OBJECTIVE: The student will analyze information by listing the supporting details of a main idea.

Reproduce and distribute Student Activity 4. Tell students that they will use this diagram to show how the American Revolution changed American politics and society. Students are to read Section 4 on pages 147–152. As they read, they are to list three ways American politics and society changed as a result of the American Revolution.

Answers to Student Activity 4

Answers will vary but students should reference three of the following: ties to the king of England were severed and a republic was established; all citizens became equal under the law; government derives authority from the people; each state's constitution should be written down and should limit government's power over the people; government needed checks and balances, separation of powers, two-house legislature, bill of rights; expansion of voting rights; government should not aid churches; schools for girls founded; more women learned to read; thousands of enslaved African Americans gained freedom; Loyalists fled the United States; nationalism increased; universities were founded; American-centered style of teaching instituted in schools.

The American Revolution, 1754–1783   **GRAPHIC ORGANIZER ACTIVITY 4**

The American Revolution and American Society

Directions: Read about the changes in American politics and society brought about by the American Revolution in Section 4 on pages 147–152 in your textbook. As you read, list three changes in American society that occurred as a result of the American Revolution.

The American Revolution changed American politics and society in many ways.

Use with Chapter 5

Problem-Solution Chart
Teaching Strategy *(Use with Section 1)*

OBJECTIVE: The student will recognize problems and describe their solutions.

⟹ Use with Graphic Organizer 12—Problem-Solution Chart—from the Graphic Organizer Library.

- Present Graphic Organizer Transparency 12 or reproduce Graphic Organizer 12. Tell students that they will use this chart to describe problems that faced the newly formed United States.
- Tell students to read "The Congress Falters" in Section 1, pages 159–162. They are to write the problems facing the newly formed United States and the solutions to each of these problems.
- Discuss with students the problems facing the newly formed United States and whether the solutions applied to these problems were successful.

PRESENTING STUDENT ACTIVITY 5
Venn Diagram Teaching Strategy and Student Activity *(Use with Section 2)*

⟹ Please note: The Venn Diagram Teaching Strategy corresponds with Graphic Organizer 5, found in the Graphic Organizer Library.

OBJECTIVE: The student will analyze information by comparing and contrasting.

Reproduce and distribute Student Activity 5. Ask students to look over the Venn diagram. Let students know that they will use this diagram to compare and contrast the New Jersey and the Virginia plans for a new national government. As students read "The Virginia and New Jersey Plans" on page 166 in Section 2 of their textbooks, they are to list facts about each plan. Facts that are in both plans should be listed in the center oval headed "Both." Discuss these plans for a national government after students have completed their diagrams.

Answers to Student Activity 5

Virginia Plan—scrap Articles of Confederation and create new national government; give national government power to make laws binding upon the states; divide legislature into two houses; voters in each state elect members of the first house; members of the second house would be elected by the first house; in both houses the number of representatives would reflect that state's population

New Jersey Plan—modify Articles of Confederation to make central government stronger; legislature would be single house in which each state was equally represented

Both—divide government into executive, legislative, and judicial branches; central government had power to raise money through taxes and regulate trade

Table
Teaching Strategy *(Use with Section 3)*

OBJECTIVE: The student will organize information on a table.

⟹ Use with Graphic Organizer 7—Table—from the Graphic Organizer Library.

- Present Graphic Organizer Transparency 7 or reproduce Graphic Organizer 7. Tell students that tables are used to organize information.
- Have students title their tables **A Great Debate,** and then write **Federalists** in the first column and **Antifederalists** in the second column.
- Tell students to read "Federalists and Antifederalists" in Section 3, page 173. Have students list information about the issues supported by each group under the proper headings on the chart.
- After students have completed their charts, ask them to discuss which group they would have joined if they had lived during this time period in the United States. Have them explain their reason for joining the group.

Plans for a National Government

Directions: Read "The Virginia and New Jersey Plans" on page 166 in Section 2 in your textbook. As you read, list key facts about each type of plan for creating a new national government. Facts that apply to both plans should be written in the center oval under the heading "Both."

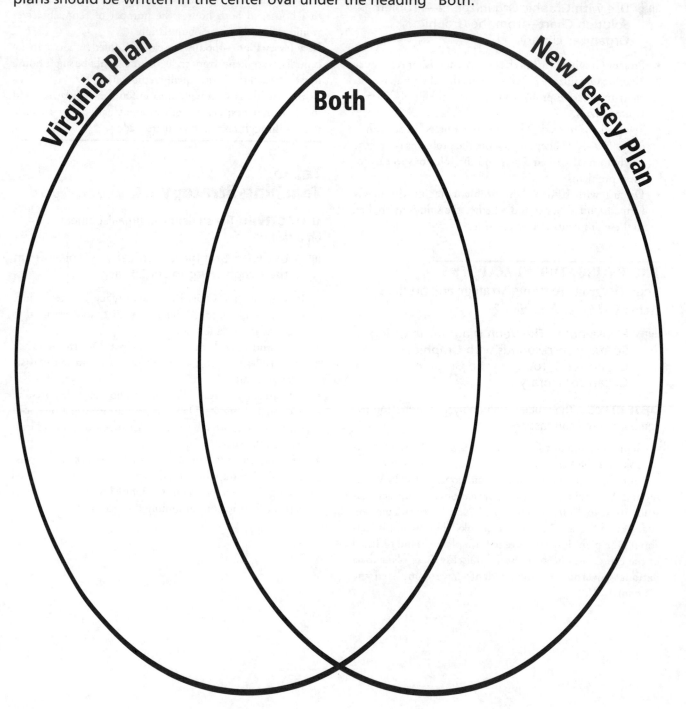

Graphic Organizer Strategies

Use with Chapter 6

Fishbone Diagram
Teaching Strategy *(Use with Section 1)*

OBJECTIVE: The student will organize a main idea and supporting facts.

▶ Use with Graphic Organizer 9—Fishbone Diagram—from the Graphic Organizer Library.

- Present Graphic Organizer Transparency 9 or reproduce Graphic Organizer 9. Tell students that fishbone diagrams are used to organize main ideas and supporting facts.
- Tell students to write the main idea, **Hamilton's Arguments for a National Bank,** on the single line on the left of the diagram. Have students read "The Bank of the United States" in Section 1, pages 212–213.
- As students read, tell them to list three arguments for creating a national bank on the right of the diagram. Discuss with students whether Hamilton's arguments were reason enough to create a national bank.

PRESENTING STUDENT ACTIVITY 6

Table or Matrix Teaching Strategy and Student Activity *(Use with Sections 2 and 3)*

▶ Please note: The Table or Matrix Teaching Strategy corresponds with Graphic Organizer 6, found in the Graphic Organizer Library.

OBJECTIVE: The student will locate information from the text and categorize the information in a table or matrix.

Reproduce and distribute Student Activity 6. Tell students that they will use this table to list key facts about the challenges facing Washington, Adams, and Jefferson during their presidencies. As students read sections 2 and 3 on pages 215–225, they are to list key facts under the headings on the table. After students have completed the tables, discuss the most crucial facts in each presidency.

Answers to Student Activity 6
Washington—war between France and Great Britain meant he had to choose sides or try to avoid war; British forts in American territory; British seized American ships; Jay's Treaty with Britain; Pinckney's Treaty with Spain; confrontations with Native Americans
Adams—French stopped American ships and seized goods going to Britain; French tried to bribe American negotiators

in XYZ Affair; Quasi-War with France; Federalists pushed Alien and Sedition Acts through Congress; Republicans pushed Virginia and Kentucky Resolutions
Jefferson—repealed Judiciary Act of 1801 to eliminate "midnight judges;" *Marbury* v. *Madison;* Louisiana Territory; keeping United States out of war between France and Great Britain; impressment by British and attack on *Chesapeake;* Embargo Act of 1807

K-W-L-H Chart
Teaching Strategy *(Use with Section 3)*

OBJECTIVE: The students will list information they know, discover what information they do not know, and then learn that new information.

▶ Use with Graphic Organizer 2—K-W-L-H Chart—from the Graphic Organizer Library.

- Present Graphic Organizer Transparency 2 or reproduce Graphic Organizer 2. Tell students that they will list information they already know on this chart. Then they will list and find the information that they do not already know.
- Tell students to list what they know about the Louisiana Purchase under the "What I Know" column on the chart. In the next column, list questions they want to find out.
- Next, have students read "The United States Expands West" in Section 3, pages 223–224 and complete the "What I Learned" column.
- Students should complete the rest of the chart and share it with the class.

Chain-of-Events or Flowchart
Teaching Strategy *(Use with Section 4)*

OBJECTIVE: The student will identify events or steps that led to a final outcome.

▶ Use with Graphic Organizer 15—Chain-of-Events or Flowchart—from the Graphic Organizer Library.

- Present Graphic Organizer Transparency 15 or reproduce Graphic Organizer 15. Tell students that they will use this chain-of-events chart to show the events that led to the War of 1812.
- Tell students to read "The Decision for War" in Section 4, pages 228–230, and then list the events that led to the War of 1812.

Federalists and Republicans, 1789–1816 | **GRAPHIC ORGANIZER ACTIVITY 6**

Challenges Facing Early Presidents

Directions: Read Sections 2 and 3 on pages 215–225 in your textbook. As you read, list key facts about the challenges facing Washington, Adams, and Jefferson during their presidencies under the proper heading on the table. Determine the most important facts in each category.

Washington	Adams	Jefferson

The American Vision

Graphic Organizer Strategies

Use with Chapter 7

Main Idea Chart
Teaching Strategy *(Use with Section 1)*

OBJECTIVE: The student will interpret information from the text by identifying the main idea and supporting details.

▐▐▶ Use with Graphic Organizer 1—Main Idea Chart—from the Graphic Organizer Library.

- Present Graphic Organizer Transparency 1 or reproduce Graphic Organizer 1. Tell students that on this chart, they will list significant details that support the main idea: **Americans developed feelings of patriotism and national unity after the War of 1812.**
- Have students read Section 1, pages 240–244. As they read, students are to list significant details from the text that support the main idea.

PRESENTING STUDENT ACTIVITY 7
Table Teaching Strategy and Student Activity
(Use with Section 2)

▐▐▶ Please note: The Table Teaching Strategy corresponds with Graphic Organizer 7, found in the Graphic Organizer Library.

OBJECTIVE: The student will organize and categorize information to make comparisons.

Reproduce and distribute Student Activity 7. Tell students that this type of organizer will help them organize and categorize information about revolutions in transportation and industrialization in the early 1800s. Ask students to read Section 2, pages 245–250. Tell students to list four revolutions that took place in transportation under the heading "Transportation" and to list four changes that took place in industrialization under the heading "Industrialization." Discuss with students how these revolutions brought changes to the North.

Answers to Student Activity 7
Transportation: Erie Canal connected the Hudson River at Albany to Lake Erie at Buffalo; National Road—major east-west highway that reached from Cumberland, Maryland, to Wheeling, Virginia (now West Virginia); steamboats made river travel more reliable; railroads enabled trains to travel fast and go wherever track was laid

Industrialization: Manufacturing went from hand tools to large, complex machines; skilled artisans gave way to workers organized by tasks; factories replaced home-based work; manufacturers sold wares nationwide; interchangeable parts transformed one-by-one process into a factory process; telegraph quickly sent messages over long-distances

Cause-Effect Chart
Teaching Strategy *(Use with Section 3)*

OBJECTIVE: The student will analyze information by identifying cause-and-effect relationships.

▐▐▶ Use with Graphic Organizer 13—Cause-Effect Chart—from the Graphic Organizer Library.

- Present Graphic Organizer Transparency 13 or reproduce Graphic Organizer 13. Tell students that a cause-and-effect chart is used to determine cause-and-effect relationships.
- Have students write the following statement inside the cause box on their cause-effect chart: **Eli Whitney invented the cotton gin, which quickly and efficiently combed the seeds out of cotton bolls.**
- Have students read "The Southern Economy" in Section 3, pages 251–253. Ask students to write the **Effect/Cause** and **Effect** statements for each box.

Tree Diagram
Teaching Strategy *(Use with Section 4)*

OBJECTIVE: The student will analyze information by identifying the main idea and details of a reading.

▐▐▶ Use with Graphic Organizer 4—Tree Diagram—from the Graphic Organizer Library.

- Present Graphic Organizer Transparency 4 or reproduce Graphic Organizer 4. Tell students to read "The Missouri Compromise" in Section 4, pages 257–258.
- Have students list three provisions of the Missouri Compromise in the three lower boxes on the tree. Then ask students to select a title for the tree and write it in the large box at the top.

GRAPHIC ORGANIZER ACTIVITY 7

Revolutions Cause Change

Directions: Read about the revolutions that took place in transportation and industrialization in Section 2 on pages 245–250 in your textbook. As you read, list four revolutions that took place in transportation under the heading "Transportation" and list four changes that took place in industrialization under the heading "Industrialization."

Transportation	Industrialization

Graphic Organizer Strategies

Use with Chapter 8

PRESENTING STUDENT ACTIVITY 8

Table: Pyramid Teaching Strategy and Student Activity *(Use with Section 1)*

▪▪▪▶ Please note: The Table: Pyramid Teaching Strategy corresponds with Graphic Organizer 8, found in the Graphic Organizer Library.

OBJECTIVE: The student will identify important facts and details from the text that have an impact on a climax, culminating, or important event.

Reproduce and distribute Student Activity 8. Tell students that they will use this pyramid to show the factors that led to the removal of most Native Americans east of the Mississippi River. Ask students to read "Policies Toward Native Americans" in Section 1, pages 269–270. As students read, ask them to identify four factors that led to the removal of most Native Americans east of the Mississippi River. Students should list events sequentially in their pyramid with the first event at the bottom and the last event at the top.

Answers to Student Activity 8

1. In Andrew Jackson's inaugural address, he declared his intention to move all Native Americans to the Great Plains.
2. John C. Calhoun formally proposed the removal of all Native Americans in 1823 when he was secretary of war.
3. President Jackson pushed through Congress the Indian Removal Act, which provided money for relocating Native Americans.
4. The army forced the remaining people to march to what is now Arkansas and Oklahoma in the journey known as the Trail of Tears.

Fishbone Diagram
Teaching Strategy *(Use with Section 2)*

OBJECTIVE: The student will analyze information by identifying the main idea and supporting details of a reading.

▪▪▪▶ Use with Graphic Organizer 9—Fishbone Diagram—from the Graphic Organizer Library.

- Present Graphic Organizer Transparency 9 or reproduce Graphic Organizer 9. Tell students that they will use this diagram to show the features of the religious revival that took place in the early 1800s. Have them write the title, **A Religious Revival,** on the left of the diagram.
- Tell students to read "A Religious Revival" in Section 2, pages 275–276. As students read, have them list three key features of the religious revival in America.
- Discuss the completed diagrams with the students.

Main Idea Chart
Teaching Strategy *(Use with Section 3)*

OBJECTIVE: The student will interpret information from the text by identifying the main idea and supporting details.

▪▪▪▶ Use with Graphic Organizer 1—Main Idea Chart—from the Graphic Organizer Library.

- Present Graphic Organizer Transparency 1 or reproduce Graphic Organizer 1. Tell students that on this chart, they will list significant details that support the following main idea: **Americans engaged in reform efforts in the early and mid-1800s.**
- Tell students to read Section 3, pages 278–282. As they read, students are to list significant details from the text that support the main idea.
- Discuss students' main idea charts.

K-W-L-H Chart
Teaching Strategy *(Use with Section 4)*

OBJECTIVE: The students will list information they know, discover what information they do not know, and then learn that new information.

▪▪▪▶ Use with Graphic Organizer 2—K-W-L-H Chart—from the Graphic Organizer Library.

- Present Graphic Organizer Transparency 2 or reproduce Graphic Organizer 2. Tell students that they will list information they already know about the abolitionist movement in the "What I Know" column on this chart. In the next column, have them list what they want to find out about the abolitionist movement.
- Tell students to read Section 4, pages 284–288 and complete the rest of the chart.
- Discuss completed charts with the students.

The Spirit of Reform, 1828–1845 **GRAPHIC ORGANIZER ACTIVITY 8**

Policies Toward Native Americans

Directions: Read "Policies Toward Native Americans" in Section 1, pages 269–270 of your textbook. As you read, identify four events that led to the removal of Native Americans east of the Mississippi River. List events sequentially in your pyramid with the first event at the bottom and the last event at the top.

Native Americans Removed

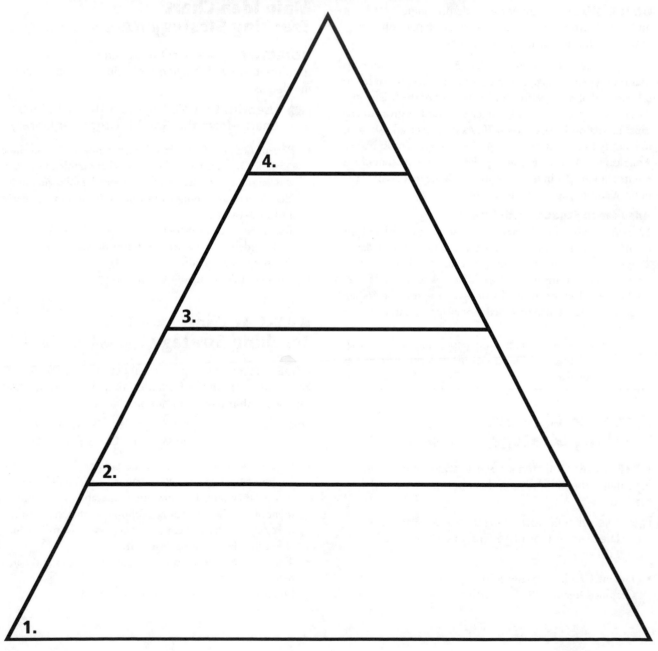

4.

3.

2.

1.

Graphic Organizer Strategies

PRESENTING STUDENT ACTIVITY 9
Fishbone Diagram Teaching Strategy and Student Activity *(Use with Section 1)*

➠ Please note: The Fishbone Diagram Teaching Strategy corresponds with Graphic Organizer 9, found in the Graphic Organizer Library.

OBJECTIVE: The student will find the main idea of a section, and then analyze the reading for further information that supports the main idea.

Reproduce and distribute Student Activity 9. Tell students that this type of fishbone diagram will help them find the main idea of a section, and they analyze the reading for further information that supports the main idea. Ask students to read "Settling the Pacific Coast" in Section 1, pages 295–297. Tell students to find information in the reading that supports the statement: **Many Challenges Faced Americans Who Moved West.** Have students list three supporting facts, one on each line on the right of the diagram. Discuss the challenges faced by Americans who moved West.

Answers to Student Activity 9
Terrain between the frontier jumping-off points and the Pacific was difficult. The typical trip west took five to six months. Travelers feared attacks by Native American warriors.

Horizontal Time Line
Teaching Strategy *(Use with Section 2)*

OBJECTIVE: The student will organize and interpret information on a time line.

➠ Use with Graphic Organizer 10—Horizontal Time Line—from the Graphic Organizer Library.

- Present Graphic Organizer Transparency 10 or reproduce Graphic Organizer 10. Tell students that they will use this time line to list important dates in the fight for Texas independence.
- Have students list the following dates on their time lines: **September 1835, December 1835, March 1836, April 1836,** and **September 1836.**
- As students read Section 2 on pages 300–304, they are to list the significance of each date on their time line.

Cause-Effect Chart
Teaching Strategy *(Use with Section 3)*

OBJECTIVE: The student will analyze information by identifying cause-and-effect relationships.

➠ Use with Graphic Organizer 13—Cause-Effect Chart—from the Graphic Organizer Library.

- Present Graphic Organizer Transparency 13 or reproduce Graphic Organizer 13. Tell students that cause-effect charts are used to analyze information by identifying cause-and-effect relationships.
- Have students write the following, **Although Mexico never recognized Texas's independence, Texas joined the Union in 1845,** in the first box on the left.
- Tell students to read Section 3, pages 306–311. As students read, ask them to write the effects of this event in the two remaining boxes.
- Discuss with students the completed cause-effect charts.

Manifest Destiny, 1835–1848

Settling the West

Directions: Find information from your text that supports the statement: **Many Challenges Faced Americans Who Moved West.** List three challenges that faced Americans who moved West, one on each line on the right of the diagram.

Many Challenges Faced Americans Who Moved West.

Graphic Organizer Strategies

Use with Chapter 10

Tree Diagram
Teaching Strategy *(Use with Section 1)*

OBJECTIVE: The student will analyze information by identifying the main idea and supporting details of a reading.

▌▌▶ Use with Graphic Organizer 4—Tree Diagram—from the Graphic Organizer Library.

• Present Graphic Organizer Transparency 4 or reproduce Graphic Organizer 4. Tell students that tree diagrams are used to record how facts are related to one another.

• Have students write the main idea, **Tensions increased between the North and the South over the question of slavery in the new states,** in the large box at the top.

• As students read Section 1, pages 320–324, have them list three details that support the main idea in the three boxes across the bottom of the diagram.

• Discuss why tensions increased between the North and the South as new states were admitted to the Union.

Chain-of-Events or Flowchart
Teaching Strategy *(Use with Section 2)*

OBJECTIVE: The student will organize and interpret information by sequencing the effects of an event.

▌▌▶ Use with Graphic Organizer 15—Chain-of-Events or Flowchart—from the Graphic Organizer Library.

• Present Graphic Organizer Transparency 15 or reproduce Graphic Organizer 15. Tell students that they will list the effects resulting from the passage of the Fugitive Slave Act. Have students write **"Fugitive Slave Act"** in the top box of their diagram.

• Tell students to read "The Fugitive Slave Act" in Section 2, pages 327–328. As they read, they are to list the chain of events following the passage of the Fugitive Slave Act in the boxes of their diagram.

• Discuss with students the consequences of the Fugitive Slave Act.

Web Diagram
Teaching Strategy *(Use with Section 3)*

OBJECTIVE: The student will identify a central idea and organize related information around it.

▌▌▶ Use with Graphic Organizer 3—Web Diagram—from the Graphic Organizer Library.

• Present Graphic Organizer Transparency 3 or reproduce Graphic Organizer 3. Tell students that web diagrams are used to identify a central idea and organize related information around it.

• Have students write the main idea, **Sectional Divisions,** in the center circle of the diagram. Tell students to read "Sectional Divisions Grow" in Section 3, pages 334–336. As students read, ask them to list and describe the sectional divisions between the North and the South in the four outer circles.

• Discuss the causes of increased divisions between the North and the South.

PRESENTING STUDENT ACTIVITY 10

Horizontal Time Line Teaching Strategy and Student Activity *(Use with Section 4)*

▌▌▶ Please note: The Horizontal Time Line Teaching Strategy corresponds with Graphic Organizer 10, found in the Graphic Organizer Library.

OBJECTIVE: The student will organize and interpret information on a time line.

Reproduce and distribute Student Activity 10. Tell students that they will use this time line to list important dates and events that led to the Civil War. As students read Section 4, pages 340–345, they are to place events and developments described in their text on the time line in chronological order. Discuss the developments that led to the Civil War with students.

Answers to Student Activity 10
Possible answers include the following:

Jun. 1860	Democratic Party split
Nov. 1860	Lincoln elected president
Feb. 1861	Six Southern states join South Carolina in secession from the Union; Confederacy formed
Mar. 1861	Lincoln inaugurated
Apr. 1861	Fort Sumter is attacked by Confederates

Sectional Conflict Intensifies, 1848–1860 | **GRAPHIC ORGANIZER ACTIVITY 10**

Events Leading Up to the Civil War

Directions: Place events and developments leading up to the Civil War on the time line below in chronological order.

**June
1860**

**June
1861**

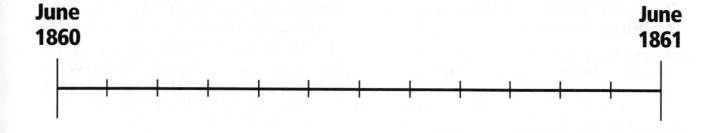

The American Vision

Graphic Organizer Strategies

Use with Chapter 11

Table
Teaching Strategy *(Use with Section 1)*

OBJECTIVE: The student will organize information on a table.

▐▐▐➡ Use with Graphic Organizer 7—Table—from the Graphic Organizer Library.

- Present Graphic Organizer Transparency 7 or reproduce Graphic Organizer 7. Tell students that tables are used to organize information.
- Tell students to title their tables, **Advantages and Disadvantages,** and write **North** in the first column and **South** in the second column.
- Read with students Section 1, pages 350–356. Have students list information about the advantages and disadvantages of the North and the South at the beginning of the Civil War.
- Ask students to review their completed tables and decide which region, North or South, had the greatest advantage at the beginning of the Civil War.

PRESENTING STUDENT ACTIVITY 11

Vertical Time Line Teaching Strategy and Student Activity *(Use with Sections 2, 4, 5)*

▐▐▐➡ Please note: The Vertical Time Line Teaching Strategy corresponds with Graphic Organizer 11, found in the Graphic Organizer Library.

OBJECTIVE: The student will analyze information by sequencing events.

Reproduce and distribute Student Activity 11. Tell students that this type of time line will help them analyze information by ordering events in the development of the Civil War. Ask students to read Sections 2, 4, and 5. Tell students to place events and developments described in their text on the time line in chronological order. Discuss the turning points of the Civil War with the students.

Answers to Student Activity 11
Possible answers include the following:

1861 Confederates defeat Union forces at First Battle of Bull Run; Union begins blockade of Confederate ports

1862 Ironclad ships fight at sea; Union captures New Orleans; Union troops defeat Confederates at Shiloh; Confederates force Union troops to retreat at Second Battle of Bull Run; Union wins Battle of Antietam; Lincoln issues Emancipation Proclamation

1863 Union cut Confederacy in two at battle of Vicksburg; Confederates defeat Union at Chancellorsville; Union defeats Confederates at Battle of Gettysburg; Gettysburg Address; Union captures Chattanooga

1864 Union captures Atlanta; Union March to the Sea cuts path of destruction through Georgia and South Carolina

1865 Confederacy surrenders to Union

Venn Diagram
Teaching Strategy *(Use with Section 3)*

OBJECTIVE: The student will compare and contrast information by identifying similarities and differences.

▐▐▐➡ Use with Graphic Organizer 5—Venn Diagram—from the Graphic Organizer Library.

- Present Graphic Organizer Transparency 5 or reproduce Graphic Organizer 5. Tell students that Venn diagrams are used to compare and contrast information.
- Tell students to read about the effects of the Civil War on the lives of soldiers and civilians in the North and the South in Section 3, pages 364–368. Have students title their Venn diagram, **Changes Caused by the Civil War.** The heads **North** and **South** should be written in the outside circles. Under these heads, students should list effects of the war that were unique to the regions. Then in the inner circle, students should list effects of the war that the North and the South had in common.
- After students have completed their diagrams, ask them to briefly explain how the effects of the Civil War on the North and on the South were alike and how they were different.

Major Events of the Civil War

Directions: Place events and developments from the Civil War on the time line below in chronological order.

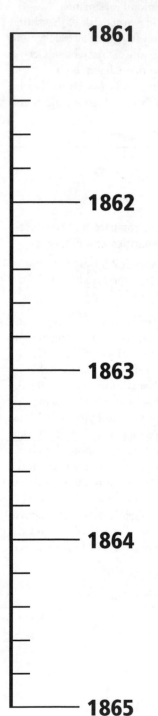

1861

1862

1863

1864

1865

Graphic Organizer Strategies

Use with Chapter 12

Main Idea Chart
Teaching Strategy *(Use with Section 1)*

OBJECTIVE: The student will interpret information from the text by identifying the main idea and supporting details.

▶ Use with Graphic Organizer 1—Main Idea Chart—from the Graphic Organizer Library.

- Present Graphic Organizer Transparency 1 or reproduce Graphic Organizer 1. Tell students that on this chart they will list significant details that support the following main idea: **In the months after the Civil War, the nation began the effort to rebuild and reunite.**
- Tell students to read Section 1, pages 386–389. As they read, students are to list significant details from the text that support the main idea.

PRESENTING STUDENT ACTIVITY 12
Problem-Solution Chart Teaching Strategy and Student Activity *(Use with Section 2)*

▶ Please note: The Problem-Solution Chart Teaching Strategy corresponds with Graphic Organizer 12, found in the Graphic Organizer Library.

OBJECTIVE: The student will recognize the problem and the written or implied solution to that problem.

Reproduce and distribute Student Activity 12. Tell students that they will use this problem-solution chart to show problems that occurred during Reconstruction, and the solutions to these problems. Have students review the problems on the chart and then read Section 2 on pages 391–395. As they read, they are to list the solutions to each of the problems.

Answers to Student Activity 12
1. Johnson implemented his Reconstruction program. He issued a new Proclamation of Amnesty; offered to pardon all former citizens of the Confederacy who took an oath of loyalty to the Union and to return their property. Each former Confederate state had to call a constitutional convention to revoke its ordinance of secession and ratify the Thirteenth Amendment.
2. Congress passed the Civil Rights Act of 1866 and introduced the Fourteenth Amendment to the Constitution to override the black codes.

3. Congress passed the Fifteenth Amendment, which declared that the right to vote "shall be denied . . . on account of race, color, or previous condition of servitude."

Web Diagram
Teaching Strategy *(Use with Section 3)*

OBJECTIVE: The student will identify a central idea and organize related information around it.

▶ Use with Graphic Organizer 3—Web Diagram—from the Graphic Organizer Library.

- Present Graphic Organizer Transparency 3 or reproduce Graphic Organizer 3. Tell students that web diagrams are used to identify a central idea and organize information around it.
- Tell students to write the main idea, **New Opportunities for African Americans,** in the center circle of the diagram. Have students read Section 3, pages 398–402. As students read, ask them to list and describe four new opportunities for African Americans under Republican rule in the South.

Venn Diagram
Teaching Strategy *(Use with Section 4)*

OBJECTIVE: The student will analyze information by comparing and contrasting.

▶ Use with Graphic Organizer 5—Venn Diagram—from the Graphic Organizer Library.

- Present Graphic Organizer Transparency 5 or reproduce Graphic Organizer 5. Tell students that they will use this Venn diagram to compare and contrast the New South and the Old South. Have them write **New South** and **Old South** in the outer circles.
- Tell students to read Section 4, pages 403–407. As students read, they are to list facts that are unique to each South in the outer circles. They should list any similarities about the New South and the Old South in the center circle.
- Review the Venn diagrams with the students.

Reconstruction, 1865–1877 **GRAPHIC ORGANIZER ACTIVITY 12**

Problems and Solutions During Reconstruction

Directions: Read Section 2 on pages 391–395 in your textbook. As you read about Reconstruction, list solutions to the problems below.

Problem

Solution

1. President Johnson wanted to bring the South back into the Union and to win Southern loyalty.

2. Southern state legislatures passed a series of black codes, which severely limited African Americans' rights in the South.

3. African Americans were denied the right to vote in many areas of the South.

The American Vision

Use with Chapter 13

Table
Teaching Strategy *(Use with Section 1)*

OBJECTIVE: The student will organize information on a table.

▐▐▐▶ Use with Graphic Organizer 7—Table—from the Graphic Organizer Library.

- Present Graphic Organizer Transparency 7 or reproduce Graphic Organizer 7. Tell students that tables are used to organize information.
- Have students write **Miners** in the first column and **Ranchers** in the second column.
- Tell students to read Section 1 on pages 414–419. Have students list and explain key terms and names that refer to Miners and Ranchers under the correct headings on the table.
- Ask students to compare the information on their tables. Than ask: How did miners and ranchers help settle the West?

PRESENTING STUDENT ACTIVITY 13

Table: Pyramid Teaching Strategy and Student Activity *(Use with Section 2)*

▐▐▐▶ Please note: The Table: Pyramid Teaching Strategy corresponds with Graphic Organizer 8, found in the Graphic Organizer Library.

OBJECTIVE: The student will identify important facts and details from the text that have an impact on a climax, culminating, or important event.

Reproduce and distribute Student Activity 13. Tell students that they will use this pyramid to identify important events that led to the settling of the Great Plains. As students read Section 2 on pages 420–423, they are to list four events

that led to the settling of the Great Plains. Discuss the pyramids with the students after completion. Ask students which event they think was most important in settling the Great Plains. Have them explain their responses.

Answers to Student Activity 13

1. Railroads provided easy access to the Great Plains.
2. The Homestead Act of 1862 provided a legal method for settlers to acquire title to property in the Great Plains.
3. New farming methods such as dry farming made farming possible and profitable on the Great Plains.
4. Inventions such as steel plows, seed drills, mechanical reapers, and threshing machines revolutionized agriculture and made dry farming possible on the Great Plains.

K-W-L-H Chart
Teaching Strategy *(Use with Section 3)*

OBJECTIVE: The students will list information they know, discover what information they do not know, and then learn that new information.

▐▐▐▶ Use with Graphic Organizer 2—K-W-L-H Chart—from the Graphic Organizer Library.

- Present Graphic Organizer Transparency 2 or reproduce Graphic Organizer 2. Tell students that they will list information they already know on this chart. Then they will list and find the information that they do not already know.
- Using the "Key Terms and Names" on page 425 of Section 3, have students list any terms and names they may already know and include a brief explanation or definition of those words.
- Have students continue work on the chart by listing "What They Want to Find Out" about the terms with which they are familiar.
- Tell students to complete the K-W-L-H chart as they read Section 3 on pages 425–430.
- Ask students to share their completed charts with the class.

GRAPHIC ORGANIZER ACTIVITY 13

Settling the Great Plains

Directions: Read Section 2 on pages 420–423 in your textbook. As you read, list four events on the pyramid that led to the settling of the Great Plains.

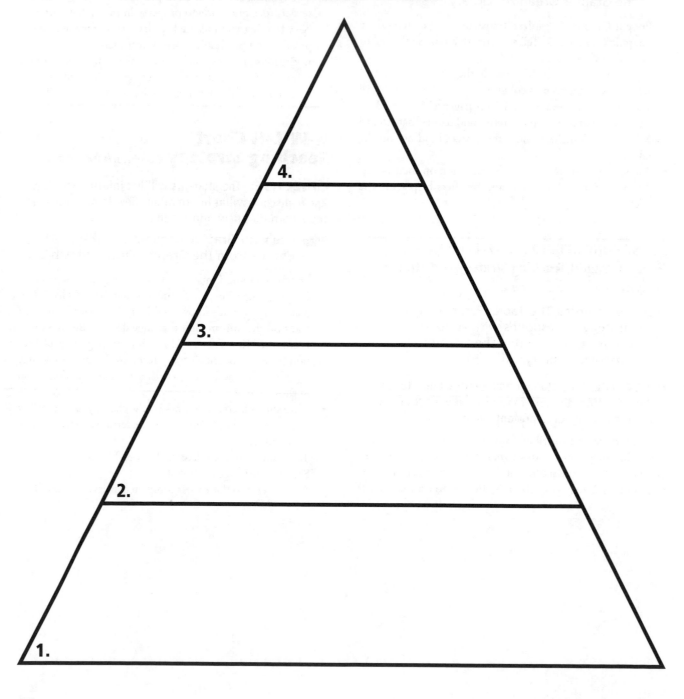

The Frontier Closes

4.

3.

2.

1.

Use with Chapter 14

PRESENTING STUDENT ACTIVITY 14

Fishbone Diagram Teaching Strategy and Student Activity *(Use with Section 1)*

▐▐▶ Please note: The Fishbone Diagram Teaching Strategy corresponds with Graphic Organizer 9, found in the Graphic Organizer Library.

OBJECTIVE: The student will find the main idea of a section, and then analyze the reading for further information that supports the main idea.

Reproduce and distribute Student Activity 14. Tell students that this type of organizer will help them find the main idea of a section, and then analyze the reading for further information that supports that main idea. Ask students to read Section 1, pages 437–440. Tell students to find information in the reading that supports the main statement: **Many Factors Led to Rapid Industrialization in the U.S. in the Late 1800s.** Have students list three supporting facts, one on each line on the right of the diagram. Discuss the completed diagram with the students.

Answers to Student Activity 14

Any three of the following: an abundance of raw materials upon which industry depended, including water, timber, coal, iron, and copper; a large population that supplied a large workforce and consumers to buy goods; free enterprise system, laissez-faire, and the profit motive, which encouraged people of high ability and ambition into business; many inventions, which increased the nation's productive capacity and improved networks of transportation and communication vital to industrial growth.

Tree Diagram
Teaching Strategy *(Use with Section 2)*

OBJECTIVE: The student will record how subordinate facts are related to one another and to a larger, unifying theme.

▐▐▶ Use with Graphic Organizer 4—Tree Diagram—from the Graphic Organizer Library.

- Present Graphic Organizer Transparency 4 or reproduce Graphic Organizer 4. Tell students that tree diagrams are used to record how subordinate facts are related to one another and to a larger, unifying theme.
- Tell students to read "Railroads Spur Growth" in Section 2,

pages 444–445. Tell students they will identify the benefits of a nationwide rail network.

- As students read, tell them to list three benefits of a nationwide rail network in the three boxes across the bottom of the diagram. Then have students write an appropriate title for the diagram in the large box at the top.
- Discuss with students the benefits of a nationwide rail network in the United States in the late 1800s. Ask students to discuss if these benefits are still the same today.

Main Idea Chart
Teaching Strategy *(Use with Section 3)*

OBJECTIVE: The student will analyze information by identifying the main idea of a reading.

▐▐▶ Use with Graphic Organizer 1—Main Idea Chart—from the Graphic Organizer Library.

- Present Graphic Organizer Transparency 1 or reproduce Graphic Organizer 1. Tell students that they will use this chart to organize information about big business in the U.S. in the late 1800s.
- Tell students to read Section 3, pages 447–451. As they read, have them first list the main idea of the section in the main idea box. Then students should list six supporting details in the appropriate boxes on the chart.
- After students have completed the main idea chart, have them summarize the text material in their own words by using the completed charts.

Chain-of-Events or Flowchart
Teaching Strategy *(Use with Section 4)*

OBJECTIVE: The student will organize and interpret information by sequencing events.

▐▐▶ Use with Graphic Organizer 15—Chain-of-Events or Flowchart—from the Graphic Organizer Library.

- Present Graphic Organizer Transparency 15 or reproduce Graphic Organizer 15. Tell students that they will use this chain-of-events flowchart to show the events that led up to the formation of unions in the late 1800s.
- Tell students to read Section 4, pages 454–459, and list events that led up to the formation of unions in the U.S. in the late 1800s on the flowchart.
- Review the completed flowcharts to make sure students have placed events in chronological order.

The Growth of Industry

Directions: Find information from your text that supports the statement:
Many Factors Led to Rapid Industrialization in the U.S. in the Late 1800s.
List three factors that led to rapid industrialization on the three lines on
the right of the diagram.

**Many Factors
Led to Rapid
Industrialization
in the U.S. in the
Late 1800s.**

Graphic Organizer Strategies

Use with Chapter 15

Tree Diagram
Teaching Strategy *(Use with Section 1)*

OBJECTIVE: The student will analyze information by identifying the main idea and supporting details of a reading.

➡ Use with Graphic Organizer 4—Tree Diagram—from the Graphic Organizer Library.

- Present Graphic Organizer Transparency 4 or reproduce Graphic Organizer 4. Tell students that tree diagrams are used to record how facts are related to one another.
- Have students write the main idea, **Immigrants enriched the culture of the United States,** in the large box at the top.
- As students read Section 1, pages 464–468, have them list three details that support the main idea in the three boxes across the bottom of the diagram.
- Discuss the contributions that immigrants made to the culture of the United States in the late 1800s.

Chain-of-Events or Flowchart
Teaching Strategy *(Use with Section 2)*

OBJECTIVE: The student will organize and interpret information by sequencing the effects of an event.

➡ Use with Graphic Organizer 15—Chain-of-Events or Flowchart—from the Graphic Organizer Library.

- Present Graphic Organizer Transparency 15 or reproduce Graphic Organizer 15. Tell students that they will list the factors that led the United States to change from a rural nation to a more urban one. Have students write **"Urbanization"** in the top box of their diagram.
- Tell students to read Section 2, pages 469–473. As they read, they are to list the factors that led the U.S. to change from a rural nation to a more urban one in the boxes of their diagram.
- Discuss with students the consequences of rapid urbanization.

Web Diagram
Teaching Strategy *(Use with Section 3)*

OBJECTIVE: The student will identify a central idea and organize related information around it.

➡ Use with Graphic Organizer 3—Web Diagram—from the Graphic Organizer Library.

- Present Graphic Organizer Transparency 3 or reproduce Graphic Organizer 3. Tell students that web diagrams are used to identify a central idea and organize related information around it.
- Have students write the main idea, **An Era of Great Cultural Change,** in the center circle of the diagram. Tell students to read Section 3, pages 476–480. As students read, ask them to list and describe the changes in American society's ideas and culture in the late 1800s in the four outer circles.
- Discuss how industrialization and urbanization led to the changes listed in the students' web diagrams.

PRESENTING STUDENT ACTIVITY 15

Horizontal Time Line Teaching Strategy and Student Activity *(Use with Section 4)*

➡ Please note: The Horizontal Time Line Teaching Strategy corresponds with Graphic Organizer 10, found in the Graphic Organizer Library.

OBJECTIVE: The student will organize and interpret information on a time line.

Reproduce and distribute Student Activity 15. Tell students that they will use this time line to list important dates and events during the reform movements of the late 1800s. As students read section 4, pages 481–486, they are to place events and developments described in their text on the time-line in chronological order. Discuss the events in the reform movements during the late 1800s.

Answers to Student Activity 15
Possible answers include the following:

1879 Henry George published *Progress and Poverty.*

1881 Booker T. Washington founded Tuskegee Institute for African Americans.

1884 Washington Gladden preached about the "right and necessity of labor organizations."

1888 Edward Bellamy published *Looking Backward, 2000–1887.*

1889 Jane Addams opened Hull House to help poor residents.

GRAPHIC ORGANIZER ACTIVITY 15

Reform Movements of the Late 1800s

Directions: Place events during the reform movements of the late 1800s on the time line below in chronological order.

1875   1880   1885   1890   1895

Graphic Organizer Strategies

Use with Chapter 16

Table
Teaching Strategy *(Use with Section 1)*

OBJECTIVE: The student will organize information on a table.

▐▐▐▶ Use with Graphic Organizer 7—Table—from the Graphic Organizer Library.

- Present Graphic Organizer Transparency 7 or reproduce Graphic Organizer 7. Tell students that tables are used to organize information.
- Tell students to title their tables **Reform Issues from 1877 to 1896,** and write **Democrats** in the first column and **Republicans** in the second column.
- Read with students Section 1, pages 492–497. Have students list information about the reform issues of the Democrats and the Republicans from 1877 to 1896.
- Ask students why only a few reforms were possible during this time period.

PRESENTING STUDENT ACTIVITY 16
Vertical Time Line Teaching Strategy and Student Activity *(Use with Section 2)*

▐▐▐▶ Please note: The Vertical Time Line Teaching Strategy corresponds with Graphic Organizer 11, found in the Graphic Organizer Library.

OBJECTIVE: The student will analyze information by sequencing events.

Reproduce and distribute Student Activity 16. Tell students that this type of time line will help them analyze information by ordering events and developments in the Populism movement. Ask students to read Section 2, pages 500–507. Tell students to place events and developments described in their text on the time line in chronological order. Discuss the main events of Populism with the students.

Answers to Student Activity 16
Possible answers include the following:
1867 The Grange formed.
1873 Congress stopped making silver coins; the U.S. was in severe recession.

1877 Farmers' Alliance began.
1886 Supreme Court ruling in *Wabash* v. *Illinois* greatly limited the states' ability to regulate railroads.
1890 People's Party, or the Populists, formed to push for political reforms.
1892 People's Party held first national convention to organize the party and nominated James B. Weaver to run for president; Democratic candidate Grover Cleveland elected president.
1893 Panic of 1893 caused the stock market to crash and banks to close. Cleveland asked Congress to repeal the Sherman Silver Purchase Act.
1896 Populists supported Democratic candidate William Jennings Bryan. However, Republican William McKinley won the election.
1900 U.S officially adopted a gold-based currency, causing Populism to lose momentum.

Fishbone Diagram
Teaching Strategy *(Use with Section 3)*

OBJECTIVE: The student will organize a main idea and supporting facts.

▐▐▐▶ Use with Graphic Organizer 9—Fishbone Diagram—from the Graphic Organizer Library.

- Present Graphic Organizer Transparency 9 or reproduce Graphic Organizer 9. Tell students that fishbone diagrams are used to organize main ideas and supporting facts.
- Tell students to write the main idea, **In the late 1800s, Southern states passed laws that denied African Americans their rights,** on the single line on the left of the diagram.
- Have students read Section 3, pages 508–512. As students read, tell them to list three laws that denied African Americans their rights on the three lines on the right of the diagram.
- Discuss with students the African American response to discrimination in Southern states.

GRAPHIC ORGANIZER ACTIVITY 16

Events Leading To and During Populism

Directions: Place events and developments leading to and during the Populism movement on the time line below in chronological order.

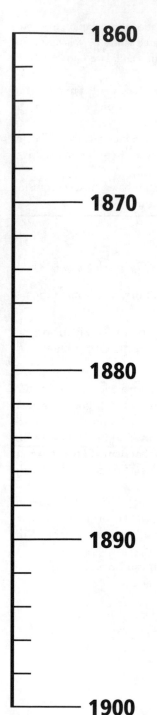

Graphic Organizer Strategies

Use with Chapter 17

Main Idea Chart
Teaching Strategy *(Use with Section 1)*

OBJECTIVE: The student will interpret information from the text by identifying the main idea and supporting details.

➠ Use with Graphic Organizer 1—Main Idea Chart—from the Graphic Organizer Library.

• Present Graphic Organizer Transparency 1 or reproduce Graphic Organizer 1. Tell students that on this chart they will list significant details that support the following main idea: **America's growing interest in world trade led to a search for territory overseas.**

• Tell students to read Section 1, pages 520–525. As they read, students are to list significant details from the text that support the main idea.

PRESENTING STUDENT ACTIVITY 17
Problem-Solution Chart Teaching Strategy and Student Activity *(Use with Section 2)*

➠ Please note: The Problem-Solution Chart Teaching Strategy corresponds with Graphic Organizer 12, found in the Graphic Organizer Library.

OBJECTIVE: The student will recognize the problem and the written or implied solution to that problem.

Reproduce and distribute Student Activity 17. Tell students that they will use this problem-solution chart to show the problems facing the United States after defeating Spain in the Spanish-American War, and the solutions to these problems.

Have students review the problems on the chart and then read Section 2 on pages 527–533. As they read, they are to list the solutions to each of the problems.

Answers to Student Activity 17
1. President McKinley decided to annex the Philippines.
2. To fight the Filipino guerrillas, American General MacArthur used many of the same policies that America had condemned Spain for using in Cuba.
3. The U.S. governor of the Philippines reformed education, transportation, and health care to help win over the Filipino people.

Table
Teaching Strategy *(Use with Section 3)*

OBJECTIVE: The student will compile and organize information on a table.

➠ Use with Graphic Organizer 7—Table—from the Graphic Organizer Library.

• Present Graphic Organizer Transparency 7 or reproduce Graphic Organizer 7. Tell students that they will use this table to show information about the Open Door Policy and the Roosevelt Corollary.

• Instruct students to label the columns with the two headings: **Open Door Policy** and **Roosevelt Corollary.**

• As students read Section 3, pages 536–541, they are to list details under the proper headings describing the foreign policies of the United States in the late 1800s and early 1900s.

• Discuss with students the effects of the two foreign policies.

Becoming a World Power, 1872–1912   **GRAPHIC ORGANIZER ACTIVITY 17**

American Imperialism in the Philippines

Directions: Read Section 2 on pages 527–533 in your textbook. As you read about the Spanish-American War, list solutions to the problems.

Problem   # Solution

1. The United States did not know what to do with the Philippines after the Spanish-American War.

2. Emilio Aguinaldo, a Filipino revolutionary leader, disagreed with annexation, and he ordered his troops to attack American soldiers in the Philippines.

3. Thousands of Filipinos died from disease and starvation in reconcentration camps set up by General MacArthur.

Graphic Organizer Strategies

Use with Chapter 18

Web Diagram
Teaching Strategy *(Use with Section 1)*

OBJECTIVE: The student will identify a central idea and organize related information around it.

▸ Use with Graphic Organizer 3—Web Diagram—from the Graphic Organizer Library.

- Present Graphic Organizer Transparency 3 or reproduce Graphic Organizer 3. Tell students that web diagrams are used to identify a central idea and organize related information around it.
- Have students write the main idea, **Political Reforms,** in the center circle of the diagram. Tell students to read "Democracy and Progressivism" in Section 1, page 549. As students read, ask them to list and describe four political reforms passed during Progressivism in the four outer circles.
- Discuss how these political reforms made the United States more democratic.

PRESENTING STUDENT ACTIVITY 18
Cause-Effect Chart Teaching Strategy and Student Activity *(Use with Section 2)*

▸ Please note: The Cause-Effect Chart Teaching Strategy corresponds with Graphic Organizer 13, found in the Graphic Organizer Library.

OBJECTIVE: The student will analyze information by identifying cause-and-effect relationships.

Reproduce and distribute Student Activity 18. Tell students that they will use this cause-effect chart to describe cause-effect relationships. Have students read Section 2, pages 555–559. As they read, students are to complete the cause-and-effect chart. Tell students to discuss their completed cause-effect charts and other progressive reforms that Theodore Roosevelt achieved during his presidency.

Answers to Student Activity 18
Cause: Theodore Roosevelt was concerned that the formation of the Northern Securities Company threatened the public interest.

Effect/Cause: Roosevelt ordered his attorney general to file a lawsuit against Northern Securities.

Effect: In *Northern Securities* v. *the United States,* the Supreme Court ruled that Northern Securities had violated the Sherman Antitrust Act. Roosevelt became known as a "trustbuster" and his popularity with the American public soared.

Fishbone Diagram
Teaching Strategy *(Use with Section 3)*

OBJECTIVE: The student will organize a main idea and supporting facts.

▸ Use with Graphic Organizer 9—Fishbone Diagram—from the Graphic Organizer Library.

- Present Graphic Organizer Transparency 9 or reproduce Graphic Organizer 9. Tell students that fishbone diagrams are used to organize main ideas and supporting facts.
- Tell students to write the main idea, **Political differences with Theodore Roosevelt caused President Taft to lose progressive support,** on the single line on the left of the diagram. Have students read Section 3 on pages 562–565.
- As students read, tell them to list and describe three political differences between Roosevelt and Taft on the three lines on the right of the diagram. Ask them to discuss the effects of the political differences between Roosevelt and Taft.

Chain-of-Events or Flowchart
Teaching Strategy *(Use with Section 4)*

OBJECTIVE: The student will identify events or steps leading up to a final outcome.

▸ Use with Graphic Organizer 15—Chain-of-Events or Flowchart—from the Graphic Organizer Library.

- Present Graphic Organizer Transparency 15 or reproduce Graphic Organizer 15. Tell students that they will use this chain-of-events chart to show how President Wilson's reforms greatly increased the federal government's role in regulating the U.S. economy.
- Tell students to read Section 4 on pages 566–570 and list reforms that increased the government's role in regulating the U.S. economy.
- Discuss students' chain-of-events charts.

The Trustbuster

Directions: After reading "Roosevelt Revives the Presidency" on pages 555–558 of Section 2 in your textbook, write the effects of the actions taken by Theodore Roosevelt.

Cause   Effect/Cause   Effect

Theodore Roosevelt was concerned that the formation of the Northern Securities Company threatened the public interest.

Graphic Organizer Strategies

Use with Chapter 19

Table: Pyramid
Teaching Strategy *(Use with Section 1)*

OBJECTIVE: The student will identify important facts and details from the text that have an impact on a climax, culminating, or important event.

➡ Use with Graphic Organizer 8—Table: Pyramid—from the Graphic Organizer Library.

- Present Graphic Organizer Transparency 8 or reproduce Graphic Organizer 8. Tell students that they will use this pyramid to show the European alliance known as the Central Powers in 1914.
- Tell students to read "Germany's Plan Fails" in Section 1 on page 580. As they read they are to list the members of the Central Powers, listing the country with the greatest power in the alliance at the top of the pyramid.
- Repeat this activity having the students show the Allied Powers and neutral nations of Europe in 1914. Ask students to read the map, "European Alliances, 1914" on page 579 of their textbook to list the members of the Allied Powers and the neutral nations. Then have the students discuss the completed pyramids and explain why the alliances developed the way they did.

Tree Diagram
Teaching Strategy *(Use with Section 2)*

OBJECTIVE: The student will analyze information by identifying the main idea and supporting details of a reading.

➡ Use with Graphic Organizer 4—Tree Diagram—from the Graphic Organizer Library.

- Present Graphic Organizer Transparency 4 or reproduce Graphic Organizer 4. Tell students that tree diagrams are used to record how facts are related to one another.
- Tell students to read Section 2 on pages 584–589. As they read, have students list three ways in which the United States had to mobilize the country for war. Have students write a title for the tree in the large box at the top.
- Ask students to share their tree diagrams with the class.

Horizontal Time Line
Teaching Strategy *(Use with Section 3)*

OBJECTIVE: The student will organize and interpret information on a time line.

➡ Use with Graphic Organizer 10—Horizontal Time Line—from the Graphic Organizer Library.

- Present Graphic Organizer Transparency 10 or reproduce Graphic Organizer 10. Tell students that they will use this time line to list important dates and events in World War I.
- As students read Section 3 on pages 592–597, have them list important dates and events during World War I.
- Ask students to explain the significance of the dates on their time lines.

PRESENTING STUDENT ACTIVITY 19

Cause-Effect Chart Teaching Strategy and Student Activity *(Use with Section 4)*

➡ Please note: The Cause-Effect Chart Teaching Strategy corresponds with Graphic Organizer 14, found in the Graphic Organizer Library.

OBJECTIVE: The student will analyze information by identifying cause-and-effect relationships.

Reproduce and distribute Student Activity 19. Tell students that this type of organizer will help them analyze information by identifying cause-and-effect relationships. Ask students to read Section 4 on pages 599–603 to complete the chart.

Answers to Student Activity 19

Cause: By the end of World War I, union membership was high, and unions were well organized. Business leaders were determined to break the power of unions and roll back union gains. **Effect:** There were enormous waves of strikes in 1919. **Cause:** Hundreds of thousands of American soldiers home from the war needed employment. Many African Americans who had moved North during the war were also competing for jobs and housing. **Effect:** Frustration and racism combined to produce violence, and in the summer of 1919, race riots broke out in over 20 northern cities. **Cause:** When the Communists withdrew Russia from World War I, they seemed to be helping Germany. Americans began to associate communism with being unpatriotic. **Effect:** Fear that Communists might seize power in the U.S. led to a nationwide panic known as the Red Scare.

World War I and Its Aftermath, 1914–1920 | GRAPHIC ORGANIZER ACTIVITY 19

Difficulties in Postwar America

Directions: As America moved to peacetime after World War I, difficulties emerged in the readjustment period. After reading Section 4 on pages 599–603 in your textbook, write the effect of each adjustment.

Causes

Effects

By the end of World War I, union membership was high, and unions were well organized. Business leaders were determined to break the power of unions and roll back union gains. 	
Hundreds of thousands of American soldiers home from the war needed employment. Many African Americans who had moved North during the war were also competing for jobs and housing.	
When the Communists withdrew Russia from World War I, they seemed to be helping Germany. Americans began to associate communism with being unpatriotic and disloyal.	

Graphic Organizer Strategies

Use with Chapter 20

Table or Matrix
Teaching Strategy *(Use with Section 1)*

OBJECTIVE: The student will categorize information in a table or matrix.

▐▐▐▶ Use with Graphic Organizer 6—Table or Matrix—from the Graphic Organizer Library.

- Present Graphic Organizer Transparency 6 or reproduce Graphic Organizer 6. Tell students that they will use this table to categorize information about the cultural movements during the 1920s.
- Students are to write the headings **Nativism, Fundamentalism,** and **Creationism** inside the heading boxes at the top of their table.
- Have students read Section 1 on pages 610–616. As they read, students are to write under each heading the definitions and list significant details from the text that describe the movement.
- Discuss the information on the table with students after completion.

Main Idea Chart
Teaching Strategy *(Use with Section 2)*

OBJECTIVE: The student will interpret information from the text by identifying the main idea and supporting details.

▐▐▐▶ Use with Graphic Organizer 1—Main Idea Chart—from the Graphic Organizer Library.

- Present Graphic Organizer Transparency 1 or reproduce Graphic Organizer 1. Tell students that on this chart, they will list significant details that support the following main idea: **The 1920s in the United States saw a dramatic increase in the country's interest in the arts and popular culture.**

- Have students read Section 2 on pages 620–623. As they read, students are to list significant details from the text that support the main idea.
- Discuss students' main idea charts after they have completed the activity. Ask them to compare today's interest in the arts and popular culture in the United States with that of the 1920s.

PRESENTING STUDENT ACTIVITY 20

Chain-of-Events or Flowchart Teaching Strategy and Student Activity *(Use with Section 3)*

▐▐▐▶ Please note: The Chain-of-Events or Flowchart Teaching Strategy corresponds with Graphic Organizer 15, found in the Graphic Organizer Library.

OBJECTIVE: The student will analyze information to identify events following an occurrence.

Reproduce and distribute Student Activity 20. Tell students that this type of organizer will help them identify events following the Great Migration of African Americans from the rural South to industrial cities in the North. As students read Section 3 on pages 626–630, they should list three events resulting from the Great Migration.

Answers to Student Activity 20
- In the New York City neighborhood of Harlem, African Americans created an environment—the Harlem Renaissance—that stimulated artistic development, racial pride, a sense of community, and political organization.
- African American writers wrote about the African American experience in the United States. African American musicians introduced jazz and blues to city nightclubs.
- African Americans became a powerful voting bloc that could sometimes sway the outcome of elections in the North.

The Jazz Age, 1921–1929   **GRAPHIC ORGANIZER ACTIVITY 20**

African American Culture

Directions: As you read Section 3 on pages 626–630 in your textbook, list the events following the Great Migration of African Americans from the rural South to industrial cities in the North.

The Great Migration

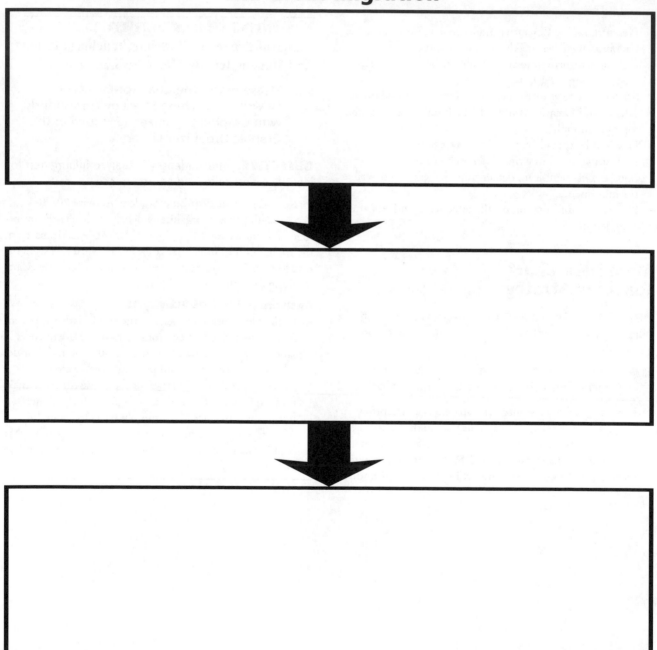

Use with Chapter 21

Table
Teaching Strategy *(Use with Section 1)*

OBJECTIVE: The student will organize information on a table.

▐▶ Use with Graphic Organizer 7—Table—from the Graphic Organizer Library.

- Present Graphic Organizer Transparency 7 or reproduce Graphic Organizer 7. Tell students that tables are used to organize information.
- Have students write **President Harding** in the first column and **President Coolidge** in the second column.
- Tell students to read Section 1, pages 636–639. As they read, have students list information about the background, politics, and administrations of each president under the appropriate heading.
- Ask students to use their tables to compare and contrast the two presidents and their administrations.

Horizontal Time Line
Teaching Strategy *(Use with Section 2)*

OBJECTIVE: The student will organize and interpret information on a time line.

▐▶ Use with Graphic Organizer 10—Horizontal Time Line—from the Graphic Organizer Library.

- Present Graphic Organizer Transparency 10 or reproduce Graphic Organizer 10. Tell students that they will use this time line to list important dates and events in the 1920s.
- As students read Section 2 on pages 640–646, have them place dates and their events and developments described in their textbook on the timeline in chronological order.
- Ask students to explain the significance of each event and development in terms of the prosperity of the 1920s.

Main Idea Chart Teaching Strategy and Student Activity *(Use with Section 3)*

▐▶ Please note: The Main Idea Chart Teaching Strategy corresponds with Graphic Organizer 1, found in the Graphic Organizer Library.

OBJECTIVE: The student will find the main idea of a section, and then analyze the reading for further information that supports that main idea.

Reproduce and distribute Student Activity 1. Tell students that this type of main idea chart will help them find the main idea of a section, and they analyze the reading for further information that supports the main idea. Ask students to read Section 3, pages 647–650. Tell students to find information in the reading that supports the main idea: **The U.S. prosperity of the 1920s was encouraged by the government's economic policies.** Have students list six supporting facts in the six boxes. Discuss with students their completed main idea charts.

Answers to Student Activity 21
Students may reference the following: balance the budget; reduce government spending; cut taxes; encourage cooperative individualism—encourage manufacturers and distributors to form trade associations, which would voluntarily share information with the federal government; Bureau of Foreign and Domestic Commerce set up to find new markets and business opportunities for American companies; Bureau of Aviation to regulate and support airline industry.

Normalcy and Good Times, 1921–1929 | **GRAPHIC ORGANIZER ACTIVITY 21**

Economic Policies

Directions: Find information in Section 3, pages 647–650 of your text-book, that supports the main idea **"The U.S. prosperity of the 1920s was encouraged by the government's economic policies"** listed in the top box. List six supporting facts in the six boxes below.

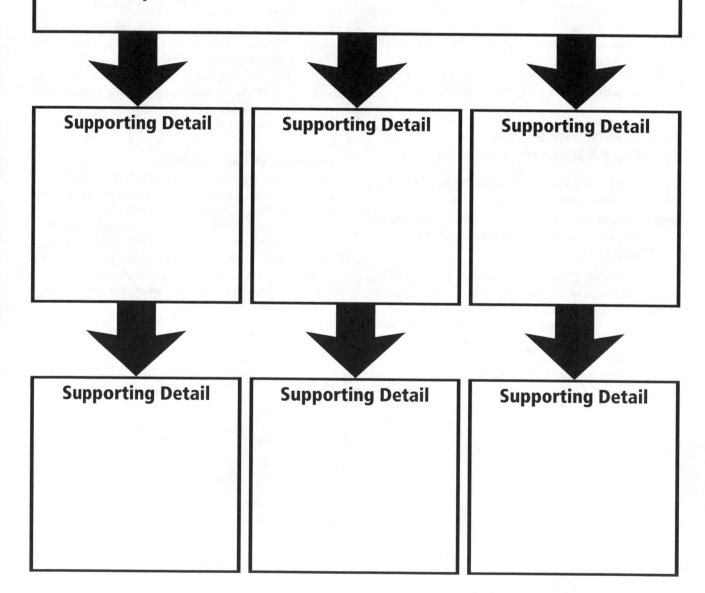

Main Idea

The U.S. prosperity of the 1920s was encouraged by the government's economic policies.

Supporting Detail

Supporting Detail

Supporting Detail

Supporting Detail

Supporting Detail

Supporting Detail

The American Vision

Graphic Organizer Strategies

Use with Chapter 22

Cause-Effect Chart
Teaching Strategy *(Use with Section 1)*

OBJECTIVE: The student will analyze information by identifying cause-and-effect relationships.

▐▐▐▶ Use with Graphic Organizer 14—Cause-Effect Chart —from the Graphic Organizer Library.

- Present Graphic Organizer Transparency 14 or reproduce Graphic Organizer 14. Tell students that they will use this cause-and-effect chart to show three causes and their effects.
- Have students read Section 1, pages 656–660. Ask them to list three causes of the Depression on the three lines on the left of the chart. Then have them list the effects of each cause on the three lines on the right of the chart.
- Discuss completed charts with the students. Ask students how the causes of the Great Depression could have been avoided.

PRESENTING STUDENT ACTIVITY 22
K-W-L-H Chart Teaching Strategy and Student Activity *(Use with Section 2)*

▐▐▐▶ Please note: The K-W-L-H Chart Teaching Strategy corresponds with Graphic Organizer 2, found in the Graphic Organizer Library.

OBJECTIVE: Students will list what they know about life during the Great Depression, discover what information they do not know, and then learn that new information.

Reproduce and distribute Student Activity 22. Tell students that they are to list what they already know about life during the Great Depression in the first column. Suggest to students that they think about the problems facing American families during the Great Depression, how they coped with those problems, and any additional facts that they may know about life during the Great Depression. In the next column they are to list what they want to find out about life during the Great Depression. Students are to complete the chart after reading Section 2 on pages 661–665 to see what they have learned about life during the Great Depression and how they can learn more. Discuss completed charts with students.

Answers to Student Activity 22
Student answers will vary. Check facts for accuracy.

Table or Matrix
Teaching Strategy *(Use with Section 3)*

OBJECTIVE: The student will categorize information in a table.

▐▐▐▶ Use with Graphic Organizer 6—Table or Matrix—from the Graphic Organizer Library.

- Present Graphic Organizer Transparency 6 or reproduce Graphic Organizer 6. Tell students that they will use this table to describe President Hoover's response to the Great Depression.
- Students are to write the heads **Recovery Plan, Goals,** and **Results** on their table.
- As students read Section 3 on pages 668–672, they are to locate the corresponding information about each recovery plan established during Hoover's administration and list that information under the proper heading.

Life During the Great Depression

Directions: List what you already know about life during the Great Depression under the "What I Know" column on the chart below. Think about the problems facing American families during the Great Depression, how they coped with those problems, and any additional facts that you may know about life during the Great Depression. In the next column list questions that you may want to find out as you read Section 2, pages 661–665 of your textbook. Complete the chart after reading Section 2 to see what you have learned about life during the Great Depression and how you can learn more.

What I Know	What I Want to Find Out	What I Learned	How Can I Learn More

Graphic Organizer Strategies

Use with Chapter 23

Tree Diagram
Teaching Strategy *(Use with Section 1)*

OBJECTIVE: The student will analyze information by identifying the main idea and supporting details of a reading.

⟹ Use with Graphic Organizer 4—Tree Diagram—from the Graphic Organizer Library.

• Present Graphic Organizer Transparency 4 or reproduce Graphic Organizer 4. Tell students that tree diagrams are used to record how facts are related to one another.

• Tell students to read Section 1 on pages 678–681. They are to list three character traits and experiences of Franklin Delano Roosevelt that prepared him for the presidency of the country during the Great Depression in the three lower boxes on the tree. Then have students write a title for the tree in the large box at the top.

• Discuss the completed diagrams with the students.

Table or Matrix
Teaching Strategy *(Use with Section 2)*

OBJECTIVE: The student will organize and categorize information in a table.

⟹ Use with Graphic Organizer 6—Table or Matrix—from the Graphic Organizer Library.

• Present Graphic Organizer Transparency 6 or reproduce Graphic Organizer 6. Tell students that they will use this table to describe the First New Deal laws.

• Students are to write the heads **First New Deal Laws, Goals,** and **Results** on their table.

• As students read Section 2 on pages 682–688, they are to locate the corresponding information about each First New Deal law established during Roosevelt's first hundred days in office and list that information under the proper heading.

PRESENTING STUDENT ACTIVITY 23
Web Diagram Teaching Strategy and Student Activity *(Use with Section 3)*

⟹ Please note: The Web Diagram Teaching Strategy corresponds with Graphic Organizer 3, found in the Graphic Organizer Library.

OBJECTIVE: The student will identify one central idea and organize related information around it.

Reproduce and distribute Student Activity 23. Tell students that they will use this web diagram to describe the Second New Deal programs. As students read Section 3 on pages 689–694 of their textbooks, they are to list and describe four Second New Deal programs. Discuss with students the results of the Second New Deal programs.

Answers to Student Activity 23
Works Progress Administration: work relief and increased employment by providing useful projects; **National Labor Relations Act (Wagner Act):** guaranteed workers the right to organize unions without interference from employers and to bargain collectively; **Rural Electrification Administration:** brought electricity to isolated agricultural areas; **Social Security Act:** created unemployment system, disability insurance, old-age pension, and child welfare benefits; **Public Utility Holding Company Act:** eliminated unfair practices and abuses of utility companies; **Banking Act:** strengthened the Federal Reserve; **Resettlement Act:** assisted poor families and sharecroppers in beginning new farms or purchasing land

Cause-Effect Chart
Teaching Strategy *(Use with Section 4)*

OBJECTIVE: The student will analyze information by identifying cause-effect relationships.

⟹ Use with Graphic Organizer 13—Cause-Effect Chart—from the Graphic Organizer Library.

• Present Graphic Organizer Transparency 13 or reproduce Graphic Organizer 13. Tell students that they will use this cause-effect chart to show the events that led up to opposition to further New Deal programs.

• Have students write **The Supreme Court declared the Agricultural Adjustment Act to be unconstitutional** in the first box on the left.

• After students have read "The Court-Packing Plan" in Section 4 on page 697, tell them to write the effects of the Supreme Court declaration of the Agricultural Adjustment Act as being unconstitutional in the two remaining boxes.

• Discuss with students the negative effects of Roosevelt's court-packing plan.

Roosevelt and the New Deal, 1933–1939   **GRAPHIC ORGANIZER ACTIVITY 23**

The Second New Deal

Directions: Read Section 3 on pages 689–694 of your textbook. As you read, list and discuss four Second New Deal programs.

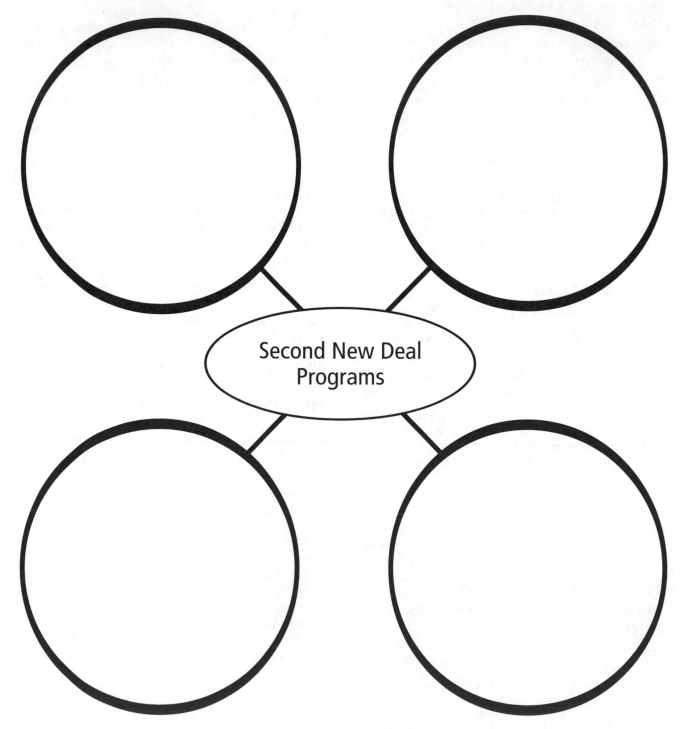

Second New Deal Programs

Use with Chapter 24

Main Idea Chart
Teaching Strategy *(Use with Section 1)*

OBJECTIVE: The student will interpret information from the text by identifying the main idea and supporting details.

▐▐▐➤ Use with Graphic Organizer 1—Main Idea Chart—from the Graphic Organizer Library.

- Present Graphic Organizer Transparency 1 or reproduce Graphic Organizer 1. Tell students that on this chart, they will list significant details that support the following main idea: **After World War I, aggressive and expansionist governments took power in both Europe and Asia.**
- Have students read Section 1 on pages 708–712. As they read, students are to list significant details from the text that support the main idea.
- Discuss students' main idea charts after they have completed the activity.

Chain-of-Events or Flowchart
Teaching Strategy *(Use with Section 2)*

OBJECTIVE: The student will identify events or steps leading up to a final outcome.

▐▐▐➤ Use with Graphic Organizer 15—Chain-of-Events or Flowchart—from the Graphic Organizer Library.

- Present Graphic Organizer Transparency 15 or reproduce Graphic Organizer 15. Tell students that they will use this chart to show the events that led up to the beginning of World War II.
- After students have read Section 2 on pages 713–718, tell them to list events that led to the beginning of World War II.
- Discuss the chain-of-events charts with students. Ask students to debate whether any of these events could have been prevented in order to have avoided World War II.

K-W-L-H Chart
Teaching Strategy *(Use with Section 3)*

OBJECTIVE: The students will list information they know, discover information they do not know, and then learn new information.

▐▐▐➤ Use with Graphic Organizer 2—K-W-L-H Chart—from the Graphic Organizer Library.

- Present Graphic Organizer Transparency 2 or reproduce Graphic Organizer 2. Tell students that they will use this K-W-L-H chart to show what they already know about the Holocaust. On their charts, have students list anything they already know about the Holocaust under the "What I Know" column, and then continue with items or questions in the second column that they may want to find out.
- After students have read Section 3 on pages 719–724, they are to complete the "What I Learned" column.
- Discuss with students how they can learn more about the Holocaust.

Tree Diagram Teaching Strategy and Student Activity *(Use with Section 4)*

▐▐▐➤ Please note: The Tree Diagram Teaching Strategy corresponds with Graphic Organizer 4, found in the Graphic Organizer Library.

OBJECTIVE: The student will analyze information by listing the supporting details of a main idea.

Reproduce and distribute Student Activity 24. Tell students that they will use this diagram to show how the United States helped Great Britain before entering World War II. Students are to read "Edging Toward War" in Section 4, pages 727–728. As they read they are to list three ways the United States helped Great Britain before entering World War II.

Answers to Student Activity 24
Lend-Lease Act: The U.S. would lend or lease arms to any country considered "vital to the defense of the United States." **Hemispheric defense zone:** the entire western half of the Atlantic was declared part of the Western Hemisphere, and therefore, neutral. Roosevelt ordered the U.S. Navy to patrol the western Atlantic and reveal the location of German submarines to the British. **Atlantic Charter:** committed the U.S. and British leaders to a postwar world of democracy.

A World in Flames, 1931–1941   **GRAPHIC ORGANIZER ACTIVITY 24**

The United States Helps Great Britain

Directions: President Roosevelt expanded the U.S. role in the war before entering World War II. Read "Edging Toward War" in Section 4 on pages 727–728 in your textbook. As you read, list three ways the United States helped Great Britain before entering World War II.

President Roosevelt expanded the U.S. role in the war by helping Great Britain before entering World War II.

The American Vision

Graphic Organizer Strategies

Use with Chapter 25

PRESENTING STUDENT ACTIVITY 25

Venn Diagram Teaching Strategy and Student Activity *(Use with Sections 1 and 3)*

➡️ Please note: The Venn Diagram Teaching Strategy corresponds with Graphic Organizer 5.

OBJECTIVE: The student will analyze information by comparing and contrasting.

Reproduce and distribute Student Activity 25. Ask students to look over the Venn diagram. Let students know that they will use this diagram to compare and contrast the roles of women before and during World War II. As students read "Women Join the Armed Forces" on page 741 in Section 1 of their textbooks and "Women in the Defense Plants" on page 750 in Section 3 of their textbooks, they are to list facts about the roles of women before World War II and facts about the roles of women during World War II. Facts about the roles of women that were true both before and during World War II should be listed in the center oval headed "Both." Discuss the completed the diagrams with the students.

Answers to Student Activity 25

Women's Roles Before World War II—Married women generally did not work outside the home. Women who did work had traditional female jobs.

Women's Roles During World War II—Women were hired for industrial jobs traditionally reserved for men—shipyards, aircraft factories, and other manufacturing plants. The army enlisted women for administrative jobs, clerical jobs, and nursing. Women joined armed forces, and some became officers in the armed forces.

Both—Women worked in the home and at traditional female jobs.

Table

Teaching Strategy *(Use with Section 2)*

OBJECTIVE: The student will organize information on a table.

➡️ Use with Graphic Organizer 7—Table—from the Graphic Organizer Library.

- Present Graphic Organizer Transparency 7 or reproduce Graphic Organizer 7. Explain the objective above.
- Have students title their tables **The Early Battles of World War II,** and write **Japan** in the first column and **Germany** in the second column.

- Tell students to read Section 2 on pages 742–747. Have students list information about the Allies' early battles of World War II under the proper headings on the chart.
- After students have completed their charts, ask them to discuss how the Allies stopped the advances of the Japanese and Germans.

Vertical Time Line

Teaching Strategy *(Use with Section 4)*

OBJECTIVE: The student will analyze information by sequencing events on a time line.

➡️ Use with Graphic Organizer 11—Vertical Time Line—from the Graphic Organizer Library.

- Present Graphic Organizer Transparency 11 or reproduce Graphic Organizer 11. Explain the objective above.
- Tell students to read Section 4 on pages 755–761. Have students write down important events and their dates on the time line. Students may want to write in pencil first so they can easily move and organize dates and events on their time lines.
- Encourage students to use their completed time lines as study guides for the chapter test.

Fishbone Diagram

Teaching Strategy *(Use with Section 5)*

OBJECTIVE: The student will organize a main idea and supporting facts.

➡️ Use with Graphic Organizer 9—Fishbone Diagram—from the Graphic Organizer Library.

- Present Graphic Organizer Transparency 9 or reproduce Graphic Organizer 9. Tell students that fishbone diagrams are used to organize main ideas and supporting facts.
- Tell students to write the main idea, **The United Nations was organized to prevent another global war,** on the single line on the left of the diagram.
- Have students read "Building a New World" in Section 5 on pages 771–772. As students read, tell them to list and describe the powers given to the United Nations to prevent global war on the three lines on the right of the diagram. Ask them to discuss the effectiveness of the United Nations.

Women's Roles Change

Directions: Read "Women Join the Armed Forces" on page 741 in Section 1 of your textbook and "Women in the Defense Plants" on page 750 in Section 3 in your textbook. As you read, list key facts about the roles of women before and during World War II. Facts that apply to roles both before and during World War II should be written in the center oval under the heading "Both."

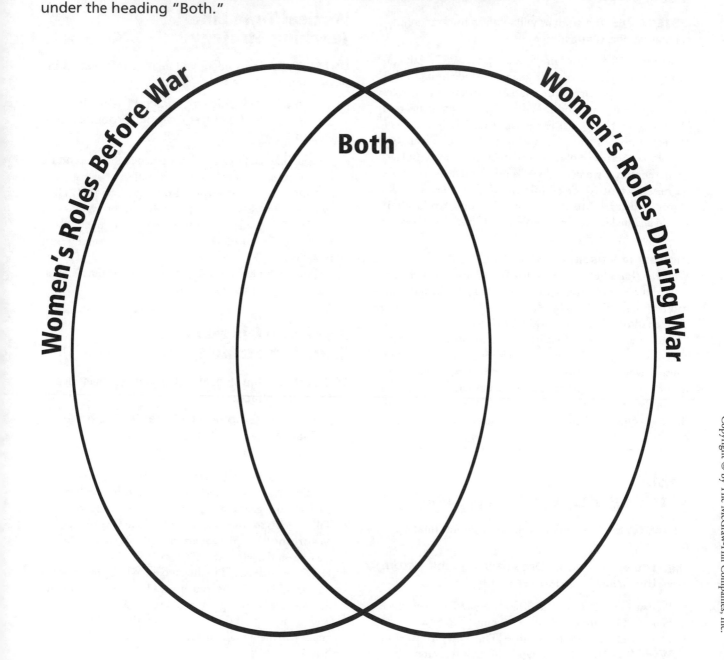

Graphic Organizer Strategies

Use with Chapter 26

Table
Teaching Strategy *(Use with Section 1)*

OBJECTIVE: The student will organize information on a table.

➤ Use with Graphic Organizer 7—Table—from the Graphic Organizer Library.

- Present Graphic Organizer Transparency 7 or reproduce Graphic Organizer 7. Tell students that tables are used to organize information.
- Have students write **Yalta Conference** in the first column and **Potsdam Conference** in the second column.
- Tell students to read Section 1, pages 778–782. As they read, have students list the outcomes of the Yalta and Potsdam Conferences under the appropriate heading.
- Ask students to use their tables to compare and contrast the outcomes of the two conferences.

PRESENTING STUDENT ACTIVITY 26
Table or Matrix Teaching Strategy and Student Activity *(Use with Section 2)*

➤ Please note: The Table or Matrix Teaching Strategy corresponds with Graphic Organizer 6, found in the Graphic Organizer Library.

OBJECTIVE: The student will locate information from the text and categorize the information in a table or matrix.

Reproduce and distribute Student Activity 26. Tell students that they will use this table to list key facts about the political, economic, and military measures used by the United States to oppose Communist aggression in Europe and Asia. Have the students read Section 2 on pages 783–789. As they read, have students list key facts about the political, economic, and military measures used by the United States to oppose Communist aggression in Europe and Asia under the proper heading on the table. After students have completed the tables, discuss the most crucial facts in each category.

Answers to Student Activity 26
Political Measures—message sent to Moscow demanding Russians withdraw from Iran; Truman Doctrine; created West Germany; NATO; used veto power in UN Security Council to keep Communist China out of UN; signed defense agreements with Japan, South Korea, Taiwan, Philippines, and Australia

Economic Measures—promised Soviets a joint Soviet-Iranian oil company if they withdrew from Iran; Marshall Plan; Berlin airlift; sent China's Nationalist government $2 billion in aid

Military Measures—USS *Missouri* sailed into the eastern Mediterranean to pressure Soviets in Iran; USS *Missouri* and aircraft carrier sent to eastern Mediterranean to protect Turkey from Soviets; Korean War; major military buildup

Chain-of-Events or Flowchart
Teaching Strategy *(Use with Section 3)*

OBJECTIVE: The student will identify events or steps that led to a final outcome.

➤ Use with Graphic Organizer 15—Chain-of-Events or Flowchart—from the Graphic Organizer Library.

- Present Graphic Organizer Transparency 15 or reproduce Graphic Organizer 15. Tell students that they will use this chain-of-events chart to show the events that led to the downfall of Senator McCarthy.
- Tell students to read "A Conspiracy So Immense" in Section 3, pages 793–795, and then to list the events that led to the downfall of Senator McCarthy.
- Ask students to discuss why McCarthyism was allowed to occur and why it ended.

Problem-Solution Chart
Teaching Strategy *(Use with Section 4)*

OBJECTIVE: The student will identify a problem and use problem-solving skills.

➤ Use with Graphic Organizer 12—Problem-Solution Chart—from the Graphic Organizer Library.

- Present Graphic Organizer Transparency 12 or reproduce Graphic Organizer 12. Tell students that they will use this chart to show problems that faced President Eisenhower and the solutions he used.
- Tell students to read Section 4 on pages 797–802. Have them identify three problems that faced President Eisenhower. Have them write the three problems in the three problem boxes. Ask students to write the solution or result of each of these problems.
- Ask students to use completed charts to discuss the effectiveness of Eisenhower's solutions.

GRAPHIC ORGANIZER ACTIVITY 26

Cold War Containment

Directions: Read Section 2 on pages 783–789 in your textbook. As you read, list key facts about the political, economic, and military measures used by the United States to oppose Communist aggression in Europe and Asia under the proper heading on the table. Determine the most important facts in each category.

Political Measures	Economic Measures	Military Measures

Graphic Organizer Strategies

Use with Chapter 27

PRESENTING STUDENT ACTIVITY 27
Table Teaching Strategy and Student Activity
(Use with Section 1)

▶ Please note: The Table Teaching Strategy corresponds with Graphic Organizer 7, found in the Graphic Organizer Library.

OBJECTIVE: The student will organize and categorize information to make comparisons.

Reproduce and distribute Student Activity 27. Tell students that this type of organizer will help them organize and categorize information about the Truman and Eisenhower administrations. Ask students to read Section 1, pages 808–813. Tell students to list four ways President Truman tried to help the nation adjust to peacetime under the heading "Truman Agenda" and to list four ways President Eisenhower tried to help the nation adjust to peacetime under the heading "Eisenhower Agenda." Have students use their tables to compare and contrast how Truman and Eisenhower tried to help the nation adjust to peacetime.

Answers to Student Activity 27
Truman Agenda: GI Bill—gave generous loans to veterans to help them establish businesses, buy homes, and attend college; halted miner's strike and railroad strike; proposed Fair Deal program: expanded Social Security benefits; raised the minimum wage; a program to ensure full employment through federal spending and investment; public housing and slum clearance; long-range environmental and public works planning; system of national health insurance; proposed civil rights legislation
Eisenhower Agenda: ended government price and rent controls; vetoed a school construction bill; slashed government aid to public housing; supported modest tax reductions; abolished RFC; slashed funding of TVA; passed the Federal Highway Act; authorized construction of Great Lakes-St. Lawrence Seaway; extended Social Security system and unemployment compensation; increased minimum wage; continued aid to farmers

Fishbone Diagram
Teaching Strategy *(Use with Section 2)*

OBJECTIVE: The student will organize a main idea and supporting facts.

▶ Use with Graphic Organizer 9—Fishbone Diagram—from the Graphic Organizer Library.

- Present Graphic Organizer Transparency 9 or reproduce Graphic Organizer 9.
- Tell students to write the main idea, **Postwar Economic Boom Brought Great Changes to American Society,** on the single line on the left of the diagram.
- Have students read Section 2 on pages 814–819. As students read, tell them to list and describe three changes to American society brought about by the postwar economic boom on the three lines on the right of the diagram.
- Ask students to discuss the completed diagrams.

Main Idea Chart
Teaching Strategy *(Use with Section 3)*

OBJECTIVE: The student will interpret information by identifying the main idea and supporting details.

▶ Use with Graphic Organizer 1—Main Idea Chart—from the Graphic Organizer Library.

- Present Graphic Organizer Transparency 1 or reproduce Graphic Organizer 1. Tell students that on this chart, they will list details that support the main idea: **During the 1950s, Americans enjoyed new forms of mass media.**
- Have students read Section 3, pages 820–825. As they read, students are to list significant details from the text that support the main idea.
- Have students create another main idea chart with the following main idea: **New and controversial styles of music and literature developed in the 1950s.**

Cause-Effect Chart
Teaching Strategy *(Use with Section 4)*

OBJECTIVE: The student will analyze information by identifying cause-and-effect relationships.

▶ Use with Graphic Organizer 13—Cause-Effect Chart—from the Graphic Organizer Library.

- Present Graphic Organizer Transparency 13 or reproduce Graphic Organizer 13.
- Have students write the following statement inside the cause box on their chart: **White middle-class families fled the cities and moved to the suburbs in the 1950s.**
- Have students read "The Decline of the Inner City" in Section 4 on page 830. Ask students to write the **Effect/Cause** and **Effect** statements for each box.

GRAPHIC ORGANIZER ACTIVITY 27

Adjustment to Peacetime

Directions: After reading Section 1, pages 808–813 in your textbook, list four ways President Truman tried to help the nation adjust to peacetime under the heading "Truman Agenda." Then list four ways President Eisenhower tried to help the nation adjust to peacetime under the heading "Eisenhower Agenda."

Truman Agenda	Eisenhower Agenda

Use with Chapter 28

Fishbone Diagram
Teaching Strategy *(Use with Section 1)*

OBJECTIVE: The student will analyze information by identifying the main idea and supporting details of a reading.

▐▐▐▶ Use with Graphic Organizer 9—Fishbone Diagram—from the Graphic Organizer Library.

- Present Graphic Organizer Transparency 9 or reproduce Graphic Organizer 9. Tell students that they will use this diagram to show the economic policies of John F. Kennedy's administration. Have them write the title **The Economic Policies of Kennedy's Administration** on the left of the diagram.
- Tell students to read "Strengthening the Economy" in Section 1, pages 842–843. As students read, have them list three key features of Kennedy's economic policies on the right of the diagram.
- Discuss the completed diagrams with the students.

Main Idea Chart
Teaching Strategy *(Use with Section 2)*

OBJECTIVE: The student will interpret information from the text by identifying the main idea and supporting details.

▐▐▐▶ Use with Graphic Organizer 1—Main Idea Chart—from the Graphic Organizer Library.

- Present Graphic Organizer Transparency 1 or reproduce Graphic Organizer 1. Tell students that on this chart, they will list significant details that support the following main idea: **Kennedy confronts the challenges and fears of the Cold War.** Have students write this main idea in the box at the top of the chart.
- Tell students to read Section 2, pages 846–851. As they read, students are to list significant details from the text that support the main idea.
- Encourage students to use this chart to help them study Section 2. Discuss students' main idea charts.

Table: Pyramid Teaching Strategy and Student Activity *(Use with Section 3)*

▐▐▐▶ Please note: The Table: Pyramid Teaching Strategy corresponds with Graphic Organizer 8, found in the Graphic Organizer Library.

OBJECTIVE: The student will identify important facts and details from the text that have an impact on a climax, culminating, or important event.

Reproduce and distribute Student Activity 28. Tell students that they will use this pyramid to show the steps President Johnson took to create the "Great Society." Ask students to read "The Great Society" in Section 3, pages 857–859. As students read, ask them to identify four Great Society programs. Students should list and describe four Great Society programs on the pyramid. Have students indicate the program that they think was the most important by placing that program at the top of the pyramid.

Answers to Student Activity 28

Students should reference any four of the following: **Medicare:** health insurance program for elderly people; **Medicaid:** health and medical assistance to low-income families; **Child Nutrition Act:** school breakfast program and expanded school lunch program and milk program; **The Elementary and Secondary Education Act:** aid to students and funded related activities such as adult education; **Higher Education Act:** supported college tuition scholarships, student loans, work-study programs for low- and middle-income students; **Project Head Start:** preschool program for disadvantaged; **The Office of Economic Opportunity:** programs to improve inner cities; **Housing and Urban Development Act:** new housing subsidy programs and federal loans and public housing grants easier to obtain; **Demonstration Cities and Metropolitan Development Act:** revitalized urban areas through social and economic programs; **Water Quality and Clean Air Acts:** supported development of standards and goals for water and air quality; **The Highway Safety Act:** supported highway safety by improving federal, state, and local coordination; **The Fair Packaging and Labeling Act:** required all consumer products to have true and informative labels

The New Frontier and the Great Society   **GRAPHIC ORGANIZER ACTIVITY 28**

Great Society Programs

Directions: Find information in "The Great Society" in Section 3, pages 857–859 of your textbook. As you read, identify and describe four Great Society programs. List the program you think was most important at the top of the pyramid.

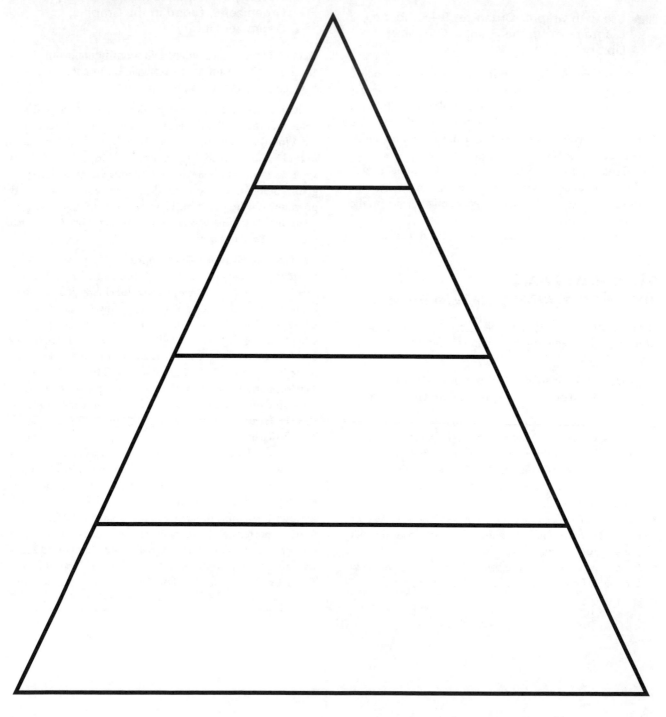

The American Vision

Graphic Organizer Strategies

Use with Chapter 29

Horizontal Time Line
Teaching Strategy *(Use with Section 1)*

OBJECTIVE: The student will organize and interpret information on a time line.

▐▐▐➡ Use with Graphic Organizer 10—Horizontal Time Line—from the Graphic Organizer Library.

- Present Graphic Organizer Transparency 10 or reproduce Graphic Organizer 10. Tell students that they will use this time line to list important dates and events in the beginning of the civil rights movement.

- As they read Section 1 on pages 866–872, students are to list the significant dates and events in the beginning of the civil rights movement on their time line.

- Discuss the dates and events with the students. Ask them to identify turning points in the civil rights movement. Remind students to refer to the time line as they study the chapter.

PRESENTING STUDENT ACTIVITY 29
Fishbone Diagram Teaching Strategy and Student Activity *(Use with Section 2)*

▐▐▐➡ Please note: The Fishbone Diagram Teaching Strategy corresponds with Graphic Organizer 9, found in the Graphic Organizer Library.

OBJECTIVE: The student will find the main idea of a section, and then analyze the reading for further information that supports the main idea.

Reproduce and distribute Student Activity 29. Tell students that this type of fishbone diagram will help them find the main idea of a section, and they analyze the reading for further information that supports the main idea. Ask students to read Section 2 on pages 873–880. Tell students to find information in the reading that supports the statement: **African American citizens and white supporters protested inequalities that African Americans faced.** Have students list three supporting facts, one on each line on the right of the diagram. Discuss with students the ways African Americans challenged segregation.

Answers to Student Activity 29
Sit-in movement staged sit-ins at places that segregated African Americans and whites. SNCC played a key role in desegregating public facilities and sent volunteers into rural areas of the Deep South to register African Americans to vote. Freedom Riders worked to integrate interstate bus service and bus terminals. Martin Luther King, Jr., launched demonstrations in Birmingham and Selma, Alabama, and a March on Washington, D.C., to push for the passage of civil rights legislation.

Problem-Solution Chart
Teaching Strategy *(Use with Section 3)*

OBJECTIVE: The student will recognize a problem and use problem-solving skills.

▐▐▐➡ Use with Graphic Organizer 12—Problem-Solution Chart—from the Graphic Organizer Library.

- Present Graphic Organizer Transparency 12 or reproduce Graphic Organizer 12. Tell students that problem-solution charts are used to analyze information by identifying problems and using problem-solving skills.

- Tell students to read Section 3, pages 881–886. As students read, ask them to write three problems and their solutions in the boxes.

- Discuss with students the completed problem-solution charts. Ask them to analyze the effectiveness of the solutions based on information in the textbook.

The Civil Rights Movement, 1954–1968   **GRAPHIC ORGANIZER ACTIVITY 29**

Civil Rights Protests

Directions: Find information from your text that supports the statement: **African American citizens and white supporters protested inequalities that African Americans faced.** After reading Section 2 on pages 873–880 in your textbook, list three supporting facts, one on each line on the right of the diagram.

African American citizens and white supporters protested inequalities that African Americans faced.

The American Vision

Graphic Organizer Strategies

Use with Chapter 30

Web Diagram
Teaching Strategy *(Use with Section 1)*

OBJECTIVE: The student will identify a central idea and organize related information around it.

▶ Use with Graphic Organizer 3—Web Diagram—from the Graphic Organizer Library.

- Present Graphic Organizer Transparency 3 or reproduce Graphic Organizer 3. Tell students that web diagrams are used to identify a central idea and organize related information around it.
- Have students write the main idea, **Reasons for U.S. Involvement in Vietnam,** in the center circle of the diagram. Tell students to read "Early American Involvement in Vietnam" in Section 1, pages 892–895. As students read, ask them to list and describe the reasons for the U.S. involvement in Vietnam in the four open circles.
- Discuss the completed web diagrams with the students.

Chain-of-Events or Flowchart
Teaching Strategy *(Use with Section 2)*

OBJECTIVE: The student will identify events or steps leading up to a final destination, conclusion, outcome, or result.

▶ Use with Graphic Organizer 15—Chain-of-Events or Flowchart—from the Graphic Organizer Library.

- Present Graphic Organizer Transparency 15 or reproduce Graphic Organizer 15. Tell students that they will list the events that deepened American involvement in Vietnam.
- Tell students to read Section 2, pages 896–901. As they read, they are to list the events that deepened American involvement in Vietnam in the boxes of their diagram.
- Discuss with students the completed chain-of-events charts. Then ask students to identify some consequences of American involvement in Vietnam.

Tree Diagram
Teaching Strategy *(Use with Section 3)*

OBJECTIVE: The student will analyze information by identifying the main idea and supporting details of a reading.

▶ Use with Graphic Organizer 4—Tree Diagram—from the Graphic Organizer Library.

- Present Graphic Organizer Transparency 4 or reproduce Graphic Organizer 4. Tell students that tree diagrams are used to record how facts are related to one another.
- Have students write the main idea, **The war in Vietnam produced sharp divisions between Americans who supported the war and those who did not,** in the large box at the top.
- As students read Section 3, pages 904–909, have them list three details that support the main idea in the three boxes across the bottom of the diagram.
- Discuss with students why tensions increased between Americans who supported the war and those who did not.

PRESENTING STUDENT ACTIVITY 30

Horizontal Time Line Teaching Strategy and Student Activity *(Use with Section 4)*

▶ Please note: The Horizontal Time Line Teaching Strategy corresponds with Graphic Organizer 10, found in the Graphic Organizer Library.

OBJECTIVE: The student will organize and interpret information on a time line.

Reproduce and distribute Student Activity 30. Tell students that they will use this time line to list important dates and events that led to the end of the Vietnam War. As students read Section 4, pages 910–914, they are to place events and developments described in their text on the timeline in chronological order. Discuss the developments that led to the end of the Vietnam War. Remind students to use the time line to help them study Chapter 30.

Answers to Student Activity 30

1969 Nixon announced the withdrawal of 25,000 American troops. Kissinger entered into negotiations with North Vietnam.

1970 Congress repealed the Gulf of Tonkin Resolution.

1971 Pentagon Papers leaked to *New York Times,* revealing the government had not been honest about the war.

1972 President Nixon dropped his longtime insistence that North Vietnamese had to withdraw from South Vietnam.

1973 The U.S. and North Vietnam signed an agreement ending the war.

The Vietnam War, 1954–1975   **GRAPHIC ORGANIZER ACTIVITY 30**

Events Leading to the End of the Vietnam War

Directions: Place events and developments leading to the end of the
Vietnam War on the time line below in chronological order.

1969   **1970**   **1971**   **1972**   **1973**

The American Vision

Graphic Organizer Strategies

Use with Chapter 31

Cause-Effect Chart
Teaching Strategy *(Use with Section 1)*

OBJECTIVE: The student will analyze information by identifying cause-effect relationships.

➠ Use with Graphic Organizer 13—Cause-Effect Chart—from the Graphic Organizer Library.

- Present Graphic Organizer Transparency 13 or reproduce Graphic Organizer 13. Tell students that they will use this cause-effect chart to identify the cause-effect relationships of the student movement and the counterculture during the 1960s.
- Have students write **Concern about the future led many young people to become more active in social causes** in the first box on the left.
- After students have read Section 1 on pages 920–925, tell them to write the effects of social activism by young people in the 1960s in the two remaining boxes.
- Discuss with students the impact of the student movement and counterculture on the United States.

PRESENTING STUDENT ACTIVITY 31
Vertical Time Line Teaching Strategy and Student Activity *(Use with Section 2)*

➠ Please note: The Vertical Time Line Teaching Strategy corresponds with Graphic Organizer 11, found in the Graphic Organizer Library.

OBJECTIVE: The student will analyze information by sequencing events.

Reproduce and distribute Student Activity 31. Tell students that this type of time line will help them analyze information by ordering events in the Feminist Movement. Ask students to read Section 2 on pages 926–930 of their textbooks. Tell students to place events and developments described in their textbooks on the time line in chronological order. Have students use their time lines to help them discuss the major achievements and failures of the women's movement.

Answers to Student Activity 31
1963 Passage of Equal Pay Act; publication of Betty Friedan's *The Feminine Mystique*

1964 Civil Rights Act, Title VII outlawed job discrimination by private employers on the basis of race, color, religion, national origin, and gender

1966 National Organization for Women (NOW) organized

1972 *Ms.* magazine published to inform of women's issues; Educational Amendments, Title IX, prohibited federally funded schools from discrimination

1973 *Roe* v. *Wade* ruled state governments could not regulate abortion during first three months of pregnancy

---

Table or Matrix
Teaching Strategy *(Use with Section 3)*

OBJECTIVE: The student will organize and categorize information in a table.

➠ Use with Graphic Organizer 6—Table or Matrix—from the Graphic Organizer Library.

- Present Graphic Organizer Transparency 6 or reproduce Graphic Organizer 6. Tell students that they will use this table to describe the new ways minority groups improved their status in the 1960s and 1970s.
- Students are to label the columns: **African Americans, Hispanics,** and **Native Americans.** On the left side of the table, outside of the table, they are to label the rows: **Leaders, Goals, Approaches,** and **Results.**
- As students read Section 3 on pages 932–937, they are to locate the corresponding information about each minority group and list that information under the proper heading.
- Ask students to compare and contrast the goals, approaches, and results of the minority groups.

Problem-Solution Chart
Teaching Strategy *(Use with Section 4)*

OBJECTIVE: The student will recognize a problem and use problem-solving skills.

➠ Use with Graphic Organizer 12—Problem-Solution Chart—from the Graphic Organizer Library.

- Present Graphic Organizer Transparency 12 or reproduce Graphic Organizer 12. Tell students that problem-solution charts are used to analyze information by identifying problems and using problem-solving skills.
- Tell students to read Section 4, pages 939–943. As students read, ask them to write three environmental problems or consumer problems and their solutions in the boxes.
- Discuss with students the completed problem-solution charts. Ask them to analyze the effectiveness of the solutions based on information in the textbook.

The Politics of Protest, 1960–1980   **GRAPHIC ORGANIZER ACTIVITY 31**

Major Events of the Feminist Movement

Directions: Place events and developments from the Feminist Movement on the time line below in chronological order.

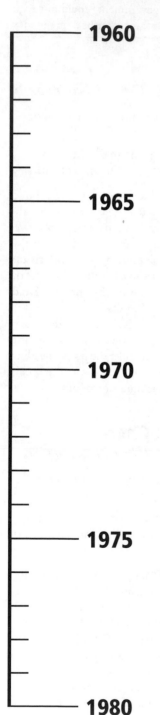

1960

1965

1970

1975

1980

Graphic Organizer Strategies

Use with Chapter 32

PRESENTING STUDENT ACTIVITY 32

Problem-Solution Chart Teaching Strategy and Student Activity *(Use with Section 1)*

▐▐▐▶ Please note: The Problem-Solution Chart Teaching Strategy corresponds with Graphic Organizer 12, found in the Graphic Organizer Library.

OBJECTIVE: The student will recognize the problem and the written or implied solution to that problem.

Reproduce and distribute Student Activity 32. Tell students that they will use this problem-solution chart to show foreign-policy problems that occurred during Nixon's administration, and the solutions to these problems. Have students review the problems on the chart and then read, "Nixon's Foreign Policy," in Section 1, pages 955–957. As they read, they are to list the solutions to each of the problems.

Answers to Student Activity 32

1. Solution: President Nixon and Henry Kissinger fashioned a foreign-policy approach called détente—relaxation of tensions between the Soviet Union and China.
2. Solution: Kissinger negotiated with Chinese leaders and Nixon visited China. The leaders of both countries agreed to establish "more normal" relations.
3. Solution: President Nixon became the first American president to visit the Soviet Union when he went to the Moscow summit. Nixon and the Soviet leader signed the Strategic Arms Limitation Treaty.

Fishbone Diagram Teaching Strategy *(Use with Section 2)*

OBJECTIVE: The student will organize a main idea and supporting facts.

▐▐▐▶ Use with Graphic Organizer 9—Fishbone Diagram—from the Graphic Organizer Library.

• Present Graphic Organizer Transparency 9 or reproduce Graphic Organizer 9. Explain the objective above.
• Tell students to write the main idea, **President Nixon became involved in a scandal that forced him to resign his presidency,** on the single line on the left of the diagram.
• Have students read Section 2 on pages 958–962. As students read, tell them to list and describe three facts that support the main idea.
• Have students discuss the effects of the Watergate scandal.

Venn Diagram Teaching Strategy *(Use with Section 3)*

OBJECTIVE: The student will analyze information by comparing and contrasting.

▐▐▐▶ Use with Graphic Organizer 5—Venn Diagram—from the Graphic Organizer Library.

• Present Graphic Organizer Transparency 5 or reproduce Graphic Organizer 5. Tell students that they will use this Venn diagram to compare and contrast the economic crises during the Ford and Carter administrations. Have them write **Ford** and **Carter** in the outer circles and **Both** in the inner circle.
• Tell students to read Section 3, pages 963–969. As students read, they are to list facts about the economic crises that were unique to Ford's administration and Carter's administration in the outer circles. They should list any similarities about the economic crises in both administrations in the center circle.
• Review the Venn diagrams with the students.

Main Idea Chart Teaching Strategy *(Use with Section 4)*

OBJECTIVE: The student will interpret information from the text by identifying the main idea and supporting details.

▐▐▐▶ Use with Graphic Organizer 1—Main Idea Chart—from the Graphic Organizer Library.

• Present Graphic Organizer Transparency 1 or reproduce Graphic Organizer 1. Tell students that on this chart they will list significant details that support the following main idea: **During the 1970s, American culture continued changing to reflect new trends and ideas.**
• Tell students to read Section 4, pages 970–974. As they read, students are to list significant details from the text that support the main idea.
• Ask students to compare their main idea charts. Remind students to refer to the charts to help them study the chapter.

Politics and Economics, 1971–1980   **GRAPHIC ORGANIZER ACTIVITY 32**

Foreign Policy Problems and Solutions

Directions: Read "Nixon's Foreign Policy" in Section 1, pages 955–957 in your textbook. As you read about the foreign-policy problems facing President Nixon during his administration, list solutions to the problems.

Problem   # Solution

1. During Nixon's administration, he felt that United States foreign policy needed to change toward the Soviet Union and China in the interests of world peace.

2. Since 1949, when a Communist government came to power in China, the United States had refused to recognize the Communists as legitimate rulers.

3. Nixon wanted to ease U.S.-Soviet tension.

Graphic Organizer Strategies

Use with Chapter 33

Web Diagram
Teaching Strategy *(Use with Section 1)*

OBJECTIVE: The student will identify a central idea and organize related information around it.

▷ Use with Graphic Organizer 3—Web Diagram—from the Graphic Organizer Library.

- Present Graphic Organizer Transparency 3 or reproduce Graphic Organizer 3. Explain the objective above.
- Have students write the main idea, **Conservatism Becomes a Mass Movement in America,** in the center circle of the diagram. Tell students to read "Conservatism Gains Support" in Section 1, pages 982–984. As students read, ask them to identify and describe four reasons American society moved in a conservative direction in the four outer circles.

Fishbone Diagram
Teaching Strategy *(Use with Section 2)*

OBJECTIVE: The student will organize a main idea and supporting facts.

▷ Use with Graphic Organizer 9—Fishbone Diagram—from the Graphic Organizer Library.

- Present Graphic Organizer Transparency 9 or reproduce Graphic Organizer 9. Explain the objective above.
- Tell students to write the main idea, **Reagan Adopts a New Cold War Foreign Policy,** on the single line on the left of the diagram.
- Have students read "Reagan Builds Up the Military" in Section 2, pages 988–989. As students read, tell them to list and describe three facts about Reagan's new Cold War foreign policy on the three lines on the right.
- Ask them to discuss the effects of Reagan's Cold War foreign policy on the federal budget.

K-W-L-H Chart Teaching Strategy
(Use with Section 3)

OBJECTIVE: The students will list information they know, discover what information they do not know, and then learn that new information.

▷ Use with Graphic Organizer 2—K-W-L-H Chart—from the Graphic Organizer Library.

- Present Graphic Organizer Transparency 2 or reproduce Graphic Organizer 2. Tell students that K-W-L-H charts are used to list information they know, discover what information they do not know, and then learn that new information.
- Using the "Key Terms and Names" on page 994 of Section 3, have students list any terms and names they may already know and include a brief definition or explanation of the terms and names.
- Have students continue working on the chart by listing "What They Want to Find Out" about the terms and names with which they are unfamiliar.
- The K-W-L-H chart should be completed and reviewed after completion of Section 3. Ask students what they learned about life in the 1980s, after completing the chart.

PRESENTING STUDENT ACTIVITY 33
Cause-Effect Chart Teaching Strategy and Student Activity *(Use with Section 4)*

▷ Please note: The Cause-Effect Chart Teaching Strategy corresponds with Graphic Organizer 13, found in the Graphic Organizer Library.

OBJECTIVE: The student will analyze information by identifying cause-and-effect relationships.

Reproduce and distribute Student Activity 33. Tell students that they will use this cause-effect chart to describe cause-effect relationships. Have students read "The Cold War Ends" in Section 4, pages 1002–1003. As they read, students are to complete the cause-and-effect chart. Tell students to discuss their completed charts.

Answers to Student Activity 33
Cause: By the late 1980s, the Soviet economy was suffering from years of inefficient central planning and huge expenditures on the arms race.

Effect/Cause: To save the economy, Soviet leader Mikhail Gorbachev instituted *perestroika,* or restructuring, and allowed private enterprise and profit-making. He also allowed *glasnost,* or openness, allowing people more freedom of religion and speech.

Effect: In 1989 peaceful revolutions replaced Communist rulers in Poland, Hungary, Czechoslovakia, Romania, and Bulgaria. The Berlin Wall was torn down, and East and West Germany reunited.

Resurgence of Conservatism, 1980–1992   **GRAPHIC ORGANIZER ACTIVITY 33**

The Cold War Ends

Directions: After reading "The Cold War Ends" in Section 4, pages 1002–1003 in your textbook, write the effects of the suffering Soviet economy in the late 1980s.

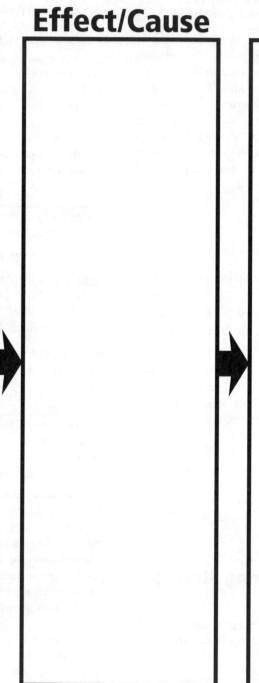

Cause   # Effect/Cause   # Effect

By the late 1980s, the Soviet economy was suffering from years of inefficient central planning and huge expenditures on the arms race.

Use with Chapter 34

Horizontal Time Line
Teaching Strategy *(Use with Section 1)*

OBJECTIVE: The student will organize and interpret information on a time line.

▶ Use with Graphic Organizer 10—Horizontal Time Line.

- Present Graphic Organizer Transparency 10 or reproduce Graphic Organizer 10. Tell students that they will use this time line to list important dates and events in the technological revolution.
- As students read Section 1 on pages 1012–1015, have them list important dates and events in the technological revolution on the time line.
- Ask students use the time line to identify the event that launched the technological revolution.

Tree Diagram
Teaching Strategy *(Use with Section 2)*

OBJECTIVE: The student will analyze information by identifying the main idea and supporting details.

▶ Use with Graphic Organizer 4—Tree Diagram—from the Graphic Organizer Library.

- Present Graphic Organizer Transparency 4 or reproduce Graphic Organizer 4. Tell students that tree diagrams are used to record how facts are related to one another.
- Tell students to read Section 2 on pages 1016–1021. As they read, have students list and describe three major economic and social reforms achieved during Clinton's presidency. Have students write a title for the tree diagram.
- Ask students to share their tree diagrams with the class.

Table
Teaching Strategy *(Use with Section 3)*

OBJECTIVE: The student will organize information on a table.

▶ Use with Graphic Organizer 7—Table—from the Graphic Organizer Library.

- Present Graphic Organizer Transparency 7 or reproduce Graphic Organizer 7.
- Have students write the title, **Growing Economic Globalization,** at the top of the table. Then have them write **Advantages** in the first column and **Disadvantages** in the second column.

- Tell students to read Section 3, pages 1022–1025. Have students list advantages and disadvantages of growing economic globalization under the appropriate heading.

PRESENTING STUDENT ACTIVITY 34

Cause-Effect Chart Teaching Strategy and Student Activity *(Use with Section 4)*

▶ Please note: The Cause-Effect Chart Teaching Strategy corresponds with Graphic Organizer 14.

OBJECTIVE: The student will analyze information by identifying cause-and-effect relationships.

Reproduce and distribute Student Activity 34. Ask students to read "A Close Vote" in Section 4, page 1028 to complete the chart. As students read, have them identify and write three cause-and-effect relationships on the chart.

Answers to Student Activity 34

Cause: The result of the 2000 election was very close in Florida. **Effect:** Florida state law required a recount of the ballots using vote-counting machines. **Cause:** Thousands of ballots had been thrown out because the counting machines could not discern a vote for president. **Effect:** Gore asked for a hand recount of ballots in several strongly Democratic counties. **Cause:** It became clear that not all of the hand recounts could be finished by the deadline. **Effect:** Gore asked the Florida Supreme Court to set a new deadline.

Fishbone Diagram
Teaching Strategy *(Use with Section 5)*

OBJECTIVE: The student will organize a main idea and supporting facts.

▶ Use with Graphic Organizer 9—Fishbone Diagram.

- Present Graphic Organizer Transparency 9 or reproduce Graphic Organizer 9.
- Tell students to write the main idea, **Middle Eastern terrorists target Americans,** on the single line on the left of the diagram.
- Have students read Section 5 on pages 1031–1037. As students read, tell them to list and describe three reasons Middle Eastern terrorists have targeted Americans on the three lines on the right of the diagram.
- Ask students to discuss their completed diagrams.

A Close Election

Directions: The election of 2000 was one of the closest in American history. After reading "A Close Vote" in Section 4, page 1028 in your textbook, identify three cause-effect relationships and write them on the chart below.

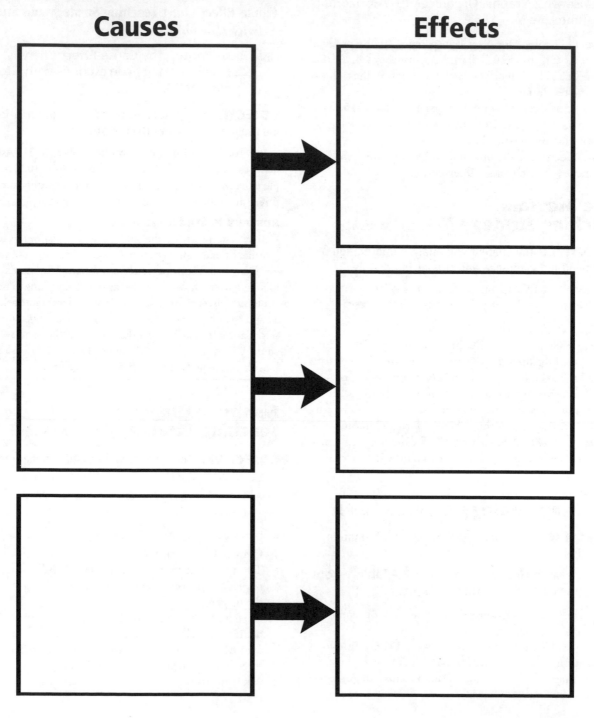

Causes   Effects